Indochina Monographs

The Easter Offensive of 1972

Lt. Gen. Ngo Quang Truong

U.S. ARMY CENTER OF MILITARY HISTORY
WASHINGTON, D.C.

Library of Congress Cataloging in Publication Data

Truong, Ngo Quang.
    The Easter offensive of 1972.

    (Indochina monographs)
    1. Easter Offensive, 1972. I. Title.
II. Series.
DS557.8.E23T78   959.704'34   79-20551

This book is not copyrighted and may be reproduced in whole or in part without consulting the publisher

Reprinted 1984

CMH PUB 92-13

Indochina Monographs

This is one of a series originally published in limited quantity in 1980 by the U.S. Army Center of Military History. The continuous demand for these monographs has prompted reprinting. They were written by officers who held responsible positions in the Cambodian, Laotian, and South Vietnamese armed forces during the war in Indochina. The General Research Corporation provided writing facilities and other necessary support under an Army contract with the Center of Military History. The monographs were not edited or altered and reflect the views of their authors--not necessarily those of the U.S. Army or the Department of Defense. The authors were not attempting to write definitive accounts but to set down how they saw the war in Southeast Asia.

These works should provide useful source materials for serious historians pending publication of the more definitive series, the U.S. Army in Vietnam.

DOUGLAS KINNARD
Brigadier General, USA (Ret)
Chief of Military History

INDOCHINA MONOGRAPHS

TITLES IN THE SERIES
(title--author/s--LC Catalog Card)

The Cambodian Incursion--Brig. Gen. Tran Dinh Tho-- CMH PUB 92-4
   79-21722

The Easter Offensive of 1972--Lt. Gen. Ngo Quang CMH PUB 92-13
   Truong--79-20551

The General Offensives of 1968-69--Col. Hoang Ngoc CMH PUB 92-6
   Lung--80-607931

Intelligence--Col. Hoang Ngoc Lung--81-10844/AACR2 CMH PUB 92-14

The Khmer Republic at War and the Final Collapse-- CMH PUB 92-5
   Lt. Gen. Sak Sutsakhan--79-607776

Lam Son 719--Maj. Gen. Nguyen Duy Hinh--79-607101 CMH PUB 92-2

Leadership--General Cao Van Vien--80-607941 CMH PUB 92-12

Pacification--Brig. Gen. Tran Dinh Tho--79-607913 CMH PUB 92-11

RLG Military Operations and Activities in the CMH PUB 92-19
   Laotian Panhandle--Brig. Gen. Soutchay
   Vongsavanh--81-10934/AACR2

The RVNAF--Lt. Gen. Dong Van Khuyen--79-607963 CMH PUB 92-7

RVNAF and U.S. Operational Cooperation and CMH PUB 92-16
   Coordination--Lt. Gen. Ngo Quang Truong--
   79-607170

RVNAF Logistics--Lt. Gen. Dong Van Khuyen-- CMH PUB 92-17
   80-607117

Reflections on the Vietnam War--General Cao Van Vien CMH PUB 92-8
   and Lt. Gen. Dong Van Khuyen--79-607979

The Royal Lao Army and U.S. Army Advice and Support-- CMH PUB 92-10
   Maj. Gen. Oudone Sananikone--79-607054

The South Vietnamese Society--Maj. Gen. Nguyen CMH PUB 92-18
   Duy Hinh and Brig. Gen. Tran Dinh Tho--79-17694

Strategy and Tactics--Col. Hoang Ngoc Lung--79-607102 CMH PUB 92-15

Territorial Forces--Lt. Gen. Ngo Quang Truong-- CMH PUB 92-9
   80-15131

The U.S. Adviser--General Cao Van Vien, Lt. Gen. Ngo CMH PUB 92-1
   Quang Truong, Lt. Gen. Dong Van Khuyen, Maj. Gen.
   Nguyen Duy Hinh, Brig. Gen. Tran Dinh Tho, Col.
   Hoang Ngoc Lung, and Lt. Col. Chu Xuan Vien--
   80-607108

Vietnamization and the Cease-Fire--Maj. Gen. Nguyen CMH PUB 92-3
   Duy Hinh--79-607982

The Final Collapse--General Cao Van Vien--81-607989 CMH PUB 90-26

Preface

In 1968, a U.S. presidential election year, Communist North Vietnam initiated the Tet Offensive, striking at almost all major cities and towns of South Vietnam. This general offensive was eventually defeated by the collective efforts of the Republic of Vietnam, United States and Free World Assistance forces. Four years later, in 1972—again a U.S. presidential election year— North Vietnam threw its entire military might behind an invasion to conquer the South. This time, however, South Vietnam had to fight for survival with only logistics and combat support provided by the United States. Almost all U.S. and Free World Military Assistance combat forces had been withdrawn when the first attacks began on 30 April 1972.

By all standards, the Easter Offensive of 1972 was one of North Vietnam's most significant initiatives during the Vietnam War. This all-out effort involved eventually in excess of ten divisions on each side and affected the lives of well over a million South Vietnamese people. During the eight long months of fierce fighting, the Republic of Vietnam Armed Forces put Vietnamization to a severe test.

During the period of the Easter Offensive, I had the privilege of participating in some of its major battles, first as IV Corps and then as I Corps commander beginning in early May 1972. I visited many of our combat units as they fought the North Vietnam Army and commanded the RVNAF counteroffensive to retake Quang Tri

City. My critical analysis of the enemy 1972 Easter Invasion, therefore, is based almost exclusively on my own personal observations, impressions and interviews with Vietnamese who were directly involved.

I am indebted to several distinguished officers of the Republic of Vietnam Armed Forces whose contributions I wish to acknowledge here. My gratitude first goes to General Cao Van Vien, Chairman of the Joint General Staff, RVNAF and my former airborne commander, who has provided me with several untold aspects of the offensive as seen from his vantage point and valuable guidance. Next, Lieutenant General Dong Van Khuyen, Commander of the Central Logistics Command, RVNAF, has contributed his unbiased comments on the joint RVNAF-US logistic effort to keep the areas under siege resupplied. Major General Nguyen Duy Hinh, who served in my corps as commander, 3d ARVN Division and who successfully rebuilt and reshaped this division into a strong combat unit, has provided me with his critical comments and judicious observations. Finally, Brigadier General Tran Dinh Tho and Colonel Hoang Ngoc Lung, the J-3 and J-2 of the Joint General Staff respectively, have contributed significant information concerning combat operations and intelligence from the JGS echelon.

Finally, I am particularly indebted to Lieutenant Colonel Chu Xuan Vien and Ms. Pham Thi Bong. Lt. Colonel Vien, the last Army Attache serving at the Embassy in Washington, D. C., has done a highly professional job of translating and editing that helps impart unity and cohesiveness to the manuscript. Ms. Bong, a former Captain in the Republic of Vietnam Armed Forces and also a former member of the Vietnamese Embassy staff, spent long hours typing, editing and in the administrative preparation of my manuscript in final form.

McLean, Virginia
31 August 1977

Ngo Quang Truong
Lieutenant General, ARVN

Contents

Chapter		Page
I.	INTRODUCTION	1
	From Insurgency to Conventional Warfare	1
	General Character of the Easter Offensive	9
II.	THE INVASION OF QUANG TRI	15
	Situation Prior to the Offensive	15
	The Initial Battles	24
	Holding The Line	31
	The Fall of Quang Tri City	41
III.	STABILIZATION AND COUNTEROFFENSIVE	48
	The Defense of Hue	48
	Refitting and Retraining	60
	Quang Tri Retaken	64
	Role of U.S. Air and Naval Support	75
IV.	DEFENDING KONTUM	78
	The NVA Force Buildup	78
	The Attacks On Tan Canh and Dakto	86
	Pressure on Kontum City	92
	The First Attack Against Kontum	95
	The Enemy's Final Attempt	101
V.	THE SIEGE OF AN LOC	106
	The Enemy's Offensive Plan in MR-3	106
	The Attack On Loc Ninh	115
	The Siege and First Attacks	116
	The Second Phase of Attack	128
	Relief from the South	131
	Mopping Up Pockets of Enemy Resistance	134

Chapter	Page
VI. ENEMY OFFENSIVE IN THE MEKONG DELTA	137
The Setting	137
Kompong Trach: The Opening Round	144
The Hau Giang Under Attack	145
Actions in the Tien Giang	149
Attacks in Dinh Tuong	151
The Aftermath	153
VII. A CRITICAL ANALYSIS	157
North Vietnam's Objectives, Strategy, and Tactics	157
The Defense Posture of South Vietnam	160
RVNAF Performance	168
U.S. Support	171
VIII. SUMMARY AND CONCLUSIONS	175
GLOSSARY	182

Maps

No.		Page
1.	The NVA General Offensive of 1972	2
2.	Key Locations and Fire Support Bases, MR-1	17
3.	NVA Attacks Across the DMZ, Quang Tri Province, 30 April 1972	26
4.	The Defense of Quang Tri, 2 April 1972	28
5.	The Shrinking 3d Infantry Division AO, Quang Tri Province	42
6.	The Defense of Hue, 5 May 1972	55
7.	Phase Lines North of Quang Tri	68
8.	Military Region 2	79
9.	Western Highlands Battlefield	84
10.	The Attack On Kontum	96
11.	Enemy Base Areas On Cambodian-RVN Border	109
12.	NVA Plan of Attacks in MR-3	111
13.	Key Locations, Binh Long Province, MR-3	113
14.	The Defense of An Loc, 12 April 1972	120
15.	The Mekong Delta, MR-4	138
16.	Enemy Base Areas in Military Region 4	140
17.	Enemy Regimental Dispositions in MR-4 (01 April 1972)	143
18.	Enemy Attacks in MR-4	147
19.	Enemy Regimental Dispositions in MR-4 (31 December 1972)	156

Illustrations

	Page
3d Division Soldier Digging In Near Dong Ha, 10 April 1972	34
A M-48 Tank of the 1st Armor Brigade Guarding Route QL-9 Near Cam Lo	35
ARVN Defensive Position on the My Chanh River	51
I Corps Forward Headquarters, Hue Citadel	52
An ARVN Antiaircraft Position Defending Hue City	58
Hue Citadel Bracing for Defense, 8 May 1972	59
President Thieu Visited the Defenses of the 1st Division	63
The Author and MG H. H. Cooksey Beside the Symbol of Victory at Quang Tri City	72
NVA 130-mm and 122-mm Artillery Captured in Quang Tri	73
Captured NVA T-54 Tank Displayed in Saigon, 14 May 1972	161
Public Display of NVA Weapons Captured During 1972 Easter Offensive	162

CHAPTER I

Introduction

From Insurgency to Conventional Warfare

On 30 March, 1972, following heavy artillery preparations, three North Vietnamese Army (NVA) divisions spearheaded by tanks crossed the Demilitarized Zone (DMZ) into South Vietnam. From the north and the west, they attacked and overran the thinly defended forward outposts and fire support bases held by the 3d Infantry Division, Republic of Vietnam Army (ARVN). Three days later, further south in Military Region 3, three other NVA divisions closed in on An Loc, 60 miles north of Saigon, after taking a district town near the Cambodian border. Then, on 14 April, two NVA divisions attacked troops of the 22d ARVN Infantry Division who manned the defenses of northwestern Kontum in Military Region 2 while directly to the east, in the lowlands of Binh Dinh Province, another NVA division struck at the province's three northern district towns. *(Map 1)*

And so, within two weeks beginning on Easter day, large conventional battles were fought simultaneously on three major fronts that pitted a total of ten NVA divisions against an equivalent number of ARVN forces. For the first time, almost the entire armored force of North Vietnam was thrown into the battles along with a significant increase in heavy artillery support. This was the largest offensive ever launched by the Communists against the Republic of Vietnam since the beginning of the war and because of enemy timing, it was quickly called the Easter invasion. Judging from the size of forces committed and the tactics employed, this offensive represented a radical departure from the methods of warfare the Communists had historically used in their attempt to conquer the South.

Map 1 – The NVA General Offensive of 1972

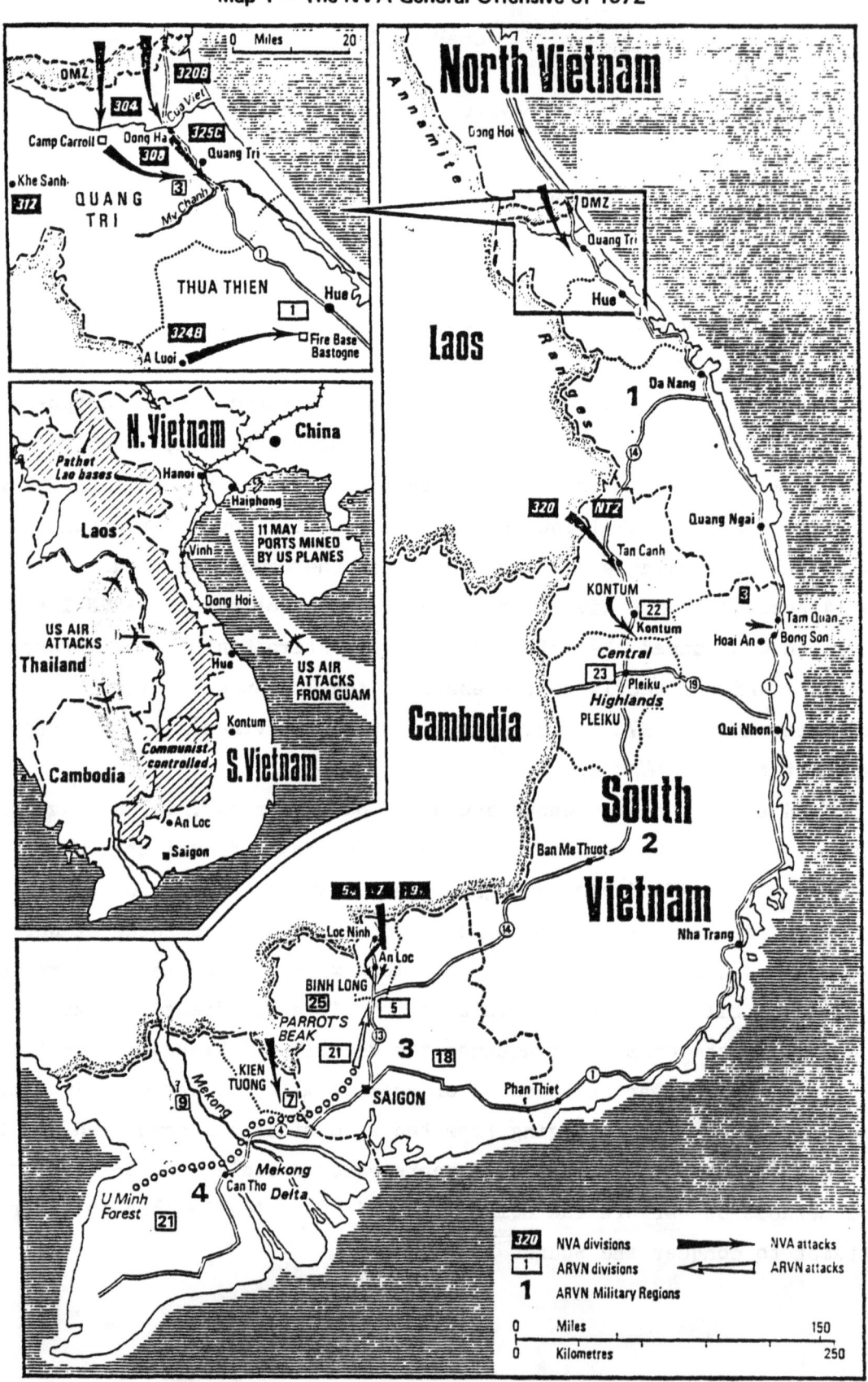

Prior to 1960, Viet Cong activities consisted primarily of small-unit attacks designed to undermine the GVN's efforts of nation-building. They were essentially hit-and-run terrorist actions, assassinations, kidnappings, and sabotage. During 1960, the first battalion-level attacks materialized. Then these attacks increased in tempo and reached multi-battalion proportions during 1961. To counter this expanding threat of insurgency, the government of Vietnam (GVN) activated additional regular units, increased the auxiliary forces (later to be called Regional and Popular or Territorial Forces), and initiated pacification efforts. At the same time, the United States also increased its military assistance to South Vietnam in terms of advisers and combat support. These concerted U.S.-RVN efforts appeared at that time to have been successful in slowing down the Communist military momentum by the end of 1962.

The political events in 1963 and the ensuing turmoil during 1964, however, seriously impeded RVN military efforts and security deteriorated rapidly. In the country side, increasing numbers of strategic hamlets were penetrated and overrun by the Viet Cong. Friendly losses in weapons increased at an alarming rate and several territorial force units in remote areas just vanished in the face of enemy pressure.

By late 1964, Viet Cong battalions had been grouped into regiments and regiments into divisions. Several large-scale battles were fought during this year; the most notable was the attack conducted by the VC 9th Division against the Catholic village of Binh Gia, east of Saigon, at year's end. During this battle, the enemy ambushed and annihilated an ARVN ranger battalion and a marine battalion. He also inflicted severe losses to an ARVN armored force which came to their relief. This was the first time enemy forces had ever remained on the battleground in sustained combat for several days. To both sides, it was an event of significant importance. The Communists considered this effort the first step toward the so-called "mobile" or final stage of their revolutionary warfare. To South Vietnam, it was the beginning of a military challenge that would be long and difficult.

In early 1965, North Vietnamese regular units began to operate in South Vietnam. The first infantry regiment to arrive, the NVA 95th, had closed into Kontum Province by the end of December the previous year. It was followed and joined by two other units, the NVA 32d and 101st Regiments, which arrived during the first two months of 1965. The enemy's objective at that time appeared to be to cut South Vietnam into two isolated halves along National Route 19 and then expand this offensive toward the completion of what he considered the decisive and possibly terminal phase of the war.

By mid-1965, ARVN forces were suffering losses which statistically amounted to an average of one battalion and one district town per week. The military situation was deteriorating at such an alarming rate, the United States deemed it necessary to commit its combat troops to fight the ground war to forestall the collapse of South Vietnam. Soon to be followed by combat units of other Free World countries, U.S. forces began to conduct search and destroy operations in August 1965. Still, the ARVN suffered another major setback at the hands of the same 9th VC Division when it reappeared at the end of the year and badly mangled the 7th ARVN Infantry Regiment in the Michelin rubber plantation north of Saigon.

As a result of the arrival and direct participation of U.S. and Free World military forces, the Republic of Vietnam Armed Forces (RVNAF) gradually regained balance. During the years 1966 and 1967, both U.S. and RVNAF units increased and expanded their offensive operations. These operations were designed primarily to destroy the enemy's bases and strongholds, clear the populated areas from his encroachment, and create a favorable setting for pacification and development. War Zones C and D, the enemy's thus far impenetrable strongholds north of Saigon and his other base areas west of Pleiku, Kontum and north of Quang Tri became targets for repeated attacks by U.S. and RVNAF units.

During this period, Communist forces operating in South Vietnam not only lost their initiative but were driven, unit by unit, away from populated centers and major areas of contest. Gradually, local Viet

Cong guerrillas became separated from their protectors, the main force units, and mutual support between these two elements was no longer as effective as it had been. As a result, the enemy's strategic posture was weakened considerably.

During 1967, the enemy endeavored to continue some of his initiatives in the Demilitarized Zone (DMZ) and in other remote areas along the national borders. But deep inside South Vietnam, there were absolutely no significant enemy activities or accomplishments. To redress this deteriorating posture, it was obvious that a major shift in effort would be required. North Vietnam leaders came to the conclusion that only a major, decisive offensive could help him turn the tide around.

Toward the end of 1967, intelligence reports began to indicate that there were significant infiltration of men and materiels and large troop movements down the Ho Chi Minh trail system and along enemy lines of communication inside South Vietnam. This information was coolly received by RVNAF authorities, more as a routine matter than a cause for alarm. Cautious measures were duly taken in the same old pattern of years past, focusing on remote areas and the countryside rather than on the cities and urban centers. As usual and routinely, a declared truce was planned during the Tet holidays commemorating the Vietnamese lunar calendar New Year.

Suddenly, the Communists initiated a general offensive, striking at almost all major cities and urban centers across the country. This occurred while the majority of Vietnamese, civilian and military alike, were celebrating the Tet amidst the deceptive quietness of the truce. From the very beginning of this offensive the enemy committed an attacking force of such proportions as never before encountered during the entire war, estimated at 84,000 troops including local forces. Attacks by fire, ground assaults, and sapper actions were repeatedly launched against 36 of the 44 provincial capitals, 5 of the 6 major cities and 64 of 242 district towns of the RVN. This was the first time that our South Vietnamese urban population had ever experienced the hazards of real war. Although taken by surprise, the RVNAF reacted swiftly and forcefully. With the support of US and Free World forces, they effectively drove off the enemy's attacks and rapidly regained control over most contested areas, with the exception of Hue, the ancient capital, and part of Saigon where it took longer to dislodge enemy troops.

In Saigon, despite their ability to penetrate the city without being detected and the fact that the defenders were caught unaware by their attacks, Communist forces were unable to occupy any key installation very long. But they clung stubbornly to the densely populous areas of Cho Lon. It took our cautious soldiers and the police forces nearly two weeks to clear the last enemy troops from the city.

At Hue after penetrating the city, Communist forces succeeded in occupying most of it, particularly the old citadel, and lay siege to several military installations. During that time, they murdered more than 3,000 defenseless servicemen and GVN civil servants and cadres stranded in the city. This 26-day battle for the control of Hue resulted in extensive destruction within the city and left 110,000 of its inhabitants homeless.

While battles were raging fiercely in cities and towns across the country, on 7 February 1968, the enemy launched determined attacks in the highland area around Khe Sanh Base near the borders of Laos and North Vietnam. This base including its airstrip, was defended by a reinforced U.S. marine regiment and an ARVN ranger battalion. Despite the enemy's repeated assaults and continuous attacks-by-fire, Khe Sanh Base held firm under siege. North Vietnam's apparent design to stage and repeat a Dien Bien Phu-type victory was soundly defeated by the overwhelming firepower of US forces.

The first phase of the enemy's general offensive of 1968 thus ended in dismal failure. The price he paid for it was excruciatingly high. Not only had he lost over 50,000 men, he had also sacrificed the elite troops of his local force in suicidal attacks. However, by bringing war into the big cities, the enemy had wrought havoc and created a resounding shock. His action also drew RVNAF and Allied forces away from the rural areas for the protection of urban centers. To deepen the psychological impact, particularly on the United States, the enemy continued his offensive campaign of 1968 with two additional phases of attack, one starting in early May and another about the middle of August. But with his forces reduced and his stamina lost, these initiatives generally ran their course until completely defeated.

After their military defeat during 1968, Communist forces in South Vietnam went through a period of decline. Despite attempts at resurgence which materialized with a country-wide offensive on 23 February 1969 and during the following two years under the form of seasonal "high point" activities, they never recovered enough to engage in large-scale and sustained attacks. As a result of his local force units being severely decimated during 1968, the enemy also had difficulties re-establishing his system of communication and mutual support between border base areas and feeder zones adjacent to urban centers. Therefore, NVA main force units in the South were virtually cut off from their usual source of supply and local guides, which were considered indispensable for effective operations.

The big challenge having been overcome, the RVNAF became more self-assured. With the strong support provided by United States and Free World Military Assistance forces, the RVNAF stepped up their operational efforts during 1969. The resulting achievements in pacification were never so good. Not only were the enemy's safe havens along the border continually under attack, his base areas inside South Vietnam, both those straddling infiltration routes and others adjacent to populous centers were also effectively "cleared and held." In August, 1969, as a result of a new policy U.S. and FWMA forces began to withdraw from South Vietnam. To help the RVNAF develop their self-contained capabilities for combat operations and pacification support, the United States undertook an accelerated program of improvement and modernization which was called Vietnamization.

All of these developments edged the Communists toward relying more on conventional methods of warfare, a radical departure from the kind of attrition warfare they had fought during the years prior to 1968. During 1970, after greatly reinforcing his forces in the South, the enemy made plans for large-scale attacks. But these plans were preempted by the Cambodian incursion during which U.S. and ARVN forces systematically destroyed almost all Communist supply bases, heretofore considered inviolable, along the border. Despite limitations imposed on it in terms of time and space, the Cambodian incursion effectively removed the threat of sustained attacks below the 12th parallel inside South Vietnam at least for one year.

Following up on their successful exploits in Cambodia, in February 1971, the RVNAF launched a large scale but limited offensive into lower Laos with substantial support in firepower, airlift and logistics provided by the United States. Code-named LAM SON 719, this operation was designed to interdict the enemy's north-south infiltration routes and to destroy his supply bases in the Tchepone area, a vital communication hub of the Ho Chi Minh trail system. ARVN forces committed in the operation were all elite, combat-proven units of the RVNAF -- the 1st Infantry, the Airborne, and the Marine Divisions. But they could not achieve all of the objectives contemplated, partly due to the forceful reactions of the enemy who for the first time employed tanks and heavy artillery in battles with success, and partly due to some tactical blunders on our part.

This experience seemed to reinforce the enemy's belief that with his modern weapons, he could defeat South Vietnam's armed forces, and consequently, the war could be ended by a military victory once U.S. troops had been withdrawn. Further, he believed that military victory could only be achieved by a conventional invasion.

To prepare for his invasion, North Vietnam requested and received huge quantities of modern weapons from Russia and Red China during 1971. These included MIG-21 jets, SAM anti-air missiles, T-54 medium tanks, 130-mm guns, 160-mm mortars, 57-mm anti-aircraft guns, and for the first time, the heat-seeking, shoulder-fired SA-7 missiles. In addition, other war supplies such as spare parts, ammunition, vehicles and fuels were shipped to North Vietnam in such amounts as never before reported during the previous years of the war.

Despite this growing military threat, the United States and other Free World allied countries maintained their disengagement policy and continued withdrawing their troops from South Vietnam at an accelerated rate. In the process, combat support assets provided by the United States for the RVNAF were also substantially reduced. As the American military presence diminished, the threat from North Vietnam became more serious. And at the beginning of 1972, it was obvious that a decisive NVA general offensive which had been in the making for some time would surely occur.

General Character of the Easter Offensive

It was not by simple coincidence that Hanoi selected the code name Nguyen Hue for its Easter invasion of 1972. Nguyen Hue was the birth name of Emperor Quang Trung, a Vietnamese national hero who in the year of the Rooster (1789) maneuvered his troops hundreds of miles through jungles and mountains from Central to North Vietnam, surprised and attacked the invading Chinese in the early days of spring and dealt them a resounding defeat in the outskirts of Hanoi.

In early 1972, Hanoi apparently wanted a repeat of this historic exploit in the other direction. But Hanoi failed to achieve the surprise that constituted the decisive advantage enjoyed by Nguyen Hue. By the end of 1971, evidences of North Vietnam's preparations for the invasion of the South had appeared from a number of sources. Notably, divisions of the NVA general reserve were moving south and a "logistics offensive" was underway in the Southern region of North Vietnam. In early December, the Joint General Staff began sending warnings to military region commanders advising them to be prepared for a major enemy attack during early 1972.

The most difficult part of the estimate concerning the enemy's obvious intention to attack was the timing. In an early warning, ARVN intelligence revealed that the enemy had the capability for a major offensive and forecast that he would probably initiate the attack sometime before the Tet or in late January. Nothing happened. Subsequently, a second estimate, based upon evidence of increased preparations in the B-3 Front, foresaw the possibility of attacks during the Tet holidays (mid-February). This warning caused the ARVN to order that troops remain in their barracks during this long holiday period; the memory of Tet 1968 was still fresh in everybody's mind. On the eve of Tet, a late decision was made to release part of the troops on the traditional three and a half days' Tet leave and the holidays passed quietly without any significant enemy-initiated activities.

Although there was general agreement in the intelligence community -- Vietnamese as well as American -- that an offensive in early 1972 was highly probable, some observers of the Vietnam scene, perhaps those not as well informed as those of us privy to the most reliable estimates, were influenced more by what seemed to them to be the illogic of a major North Vietnamese attack at this time. They reasoned that to ensure victory, North Vietnam would wait until 1973 when most, if not all, U.S. forces would have been withdrawn according to plans. It would be impossible then for the United States to re-introduce troops and the chances of U.S. intervention by air would also diminish.

To Hanoi, however, 1972 was apparently just as good an opportunity since by the end of January, U.S. combat strength in South Vietnam would have been reduced to 140,000 and should reach below 70,000 by the end of April. By that time, the remainder of U.S. forces would consist merely of three combat battalions and some tactical aircraft and helicopters, a combat force no longer considered significant. In a certain sense, this residual force would make 1972 look even more attractive in Hanoi's eyes because if it could achieve a military victory, the U.S. would certainly have to share in South Vietnam's defeat. Moreover, if the Vietnamization program and RVN pacification efforts were permitted to continue successfully and without interruption throughout the year, the military conquest of South Vietnam might well be much more difficult. To Hanoi, therefore, 1972 was the year for action.

With regard to timing, North Vietnam's genuine problem was probably to launch the invasion at such a time as to be neither too far ahead of the U.S. presidential electons in November so as to enhance its political impact nor too late into the dry season when torrential rains by late May could seriously impede movements on infiltration routes along the border. It was logical that Hanoi would want to be sure that when the fighting required large troop movements and resupplies, it would not be caught short. But if the invasion was to take place too early in the dry season and did not succeed, it would also be difficult and costly for North Vietnam to sustain its offensive drive through the rainy season. In any event, Hanoi's ultimate goal was to ensure a military victory. It did not make sense in this case to delay action any longer once preparations had been made. For one thing, a long delay would be costly logistically and morale sapping when thousands of combat troops lay idle. For another, the assembled units might well become targets for heavy strikes by the U.S. Air Force. It then became obvious that late March or early April was the best time to initiate attacks.

But where would these attacks take place and what objectives did the enemy have in mind in 1972? To veteran military intelligence officers, these questions were not very difficult to answer. Again, based on past activity patterns and geopolitical goals of the enemy they would predict that his actions would probably occur in areas where NVA main force units and their supplies were concentrated such as in the DMZ, the Tri-Border area, or in those areas adjacent to such well established base areas as War Zones C and D, Dong Thap (Plain of Reeds), and U Minh. More precisely, current intelligence on the disposition and deployment of NVA main force units at the time allowed us to estimate that in MR-1, there would be a two-pronged attack, one to be conducted by the NVA 304th and 308th Divisions from the direction of Khe Sanh against Quang Tri, and the other, an eastward effort by the NVA 324B Division from the Laotian border against Hue. The enemy's apparent objectives were to occupy Hue, the ancient capital, and threaten the harbor and airport of Da Nang, 60 miles to the south.

The second enemy effort would be directed against the highlands of MR-2 with Kontum as a primary target. This attack was to be conducted by two NVA divisions, the 2d and 320th. Farther to the south, in MR-3, it was possible that, in concert with the total effort, the three enemy divisions in that area, the 5th, 7th, and 9th, would launch attacks north of Saigon against provinces adjoining the Cambodian border such as Tay Ninh, Binh Long and Phuoc Long. Two other NVA divisions, the 3d "Gold Star" in the mountainous redoubt of northern Binh Dinh Province, and the 1st, in the Cambodian border area west of the Mekong River, and other elements in the U Minh forest area might also join in the offensive with local attacks.

Although the three areas of the enemy's major concentrations -- northern MR-1, Kontum, and north of Saigon -- were clear indicators that the heaviest attacks would occur in these regions, it was impossible, on the basis of available intelligence, to determine the priority the enemy assigned to the three objective areas. Neither could we tell which attack would be launched first, or if they would occur simultaneously.

The real issue, as far as the RVN was concerned, however, was not so much the enemy's choice of primary effort or his timing as the proportions of his offensive. It was fairly easy to predict that the invasion would dwarf all other previous attempts in scale; it was also possible to predict with reasonable accuracy how much combat force the enemy was going to commit in this invasion initially -- which in all probability would consist of at least 10 divisions and supporting elements or a total of about 130,000 troops. But no one was able to conclude at that time exactly how much reinforcement these initial forces would eventually receive in the next stage and ultimately what size the NVA total commitment would be. Obviously, it was also equally impossible to tell how long the offensive would last and finally, how much sacrifice the enemy would be prepared to accept to ensure his victory. These were the questions left unanswered until after NVA troops crossed the DMZ on 30 March, 1972.

The enemy's Nguyen Hue campaign finally materialized under the form of an unprecedented, conventional invasion with three large spearheads or efforts. The first effort was conducted across the DMZ in northern Quang Tri Province; it was combined with another effort driven eastward in the direction of Hue City. The second effort, initiated a few days later, struck into Binh Long Province in northern MR-3 from the Cambodian border. The third effort, which was conducted after initial successes in Quang Tri and Binh Long, was directed against Kontum Province in northern MR-2 at the same time as attacks in Binh Dinh Province in the coastal lowlands. The Mekong Delta, meanwhile, remained unusually quiet despite a significant increase in enemy activities, especially in some areas adjacent to the Cambodian border and in Chuong Thien Province which bordered on the U Minh forest. The enemy's effort in MR-4, however, was neither as concentrated nor as sustained as in the other military regions.

North Vietnam, as it turned out, was committing its entire combat force -- 14 divisions, 26 separate regiments, and supporting armor and artillery units -- into the battles, except the 316th Division which was operating in Laos. The fierceness of this all-out invasion turned parts of South Vietnam into a blazing inferno. The enemy's classic frontal assaults which spearheaded these battles proved tremendously effective, at least during the initial stage. Our strong-points just south of the DMZ, a responsibility of the ARVN 3d Infantry Division, were unable to hold more than three days under repeated artillery barrages and vigorous attacks by enemy armor and infantry forces. After a month of resisting, our 3d Division and the defending forces of northern MR-1 disintegrated; Quang Tri city fell into enemy hands. Areas north of Binh Long and west of Kontum were also under his control and the cities of An Loc and Kontum were under heavy attack.

It was only three months after the outbreak of the invasion that ARVN forces regained their poise supported by powerful and effective U.S. tactical air and naval gunfire, and began the counteroffensive.

The ARVN counteroffensive was fairly effective. Not only did it completely stall the NVA invasion on all major fronts, it also succeeded in recovering part of the lost territory, including the provincial capital of Quang Tri, the first ever to fall into enemy hands. This feat alone, notwithstanding the heroic seige of An Loc and the unyielding defense of Kontum, eloquently testified to the combat effectiveness of the Republic of Vietnam Armed Forces and offered proof of the success of the Vietnamization program. The biggest challenge had been met, our combat maturity had been proven, and the South Vietnamese people's self-assurance was growing. This occurred at a time when the Paris peace talks were entering the final stage. Never before had the RVN strategic posture been so good, its bargaining position so strong and its prospects of national survival so promising.

The battles fought during the blazing-red summer of 1972 marked a turning point in the Vietnam war. For the first time, Communist North Vietnam realized it had no chance of a military victory while the U.S. still provided the South with air support and adequate logistics. It was finally compelled to accept a cease-fire.

The battles of the Easter offensive, the gains and setbacks, and the strengths and weaknesses of both sides will be presented and critically analyzed in the following chapters.

CHAPTER II

The Invasion of Quang Tri

Situation Prior to the Offensive

Military Region 1 consisted of the five northern provinces of South Vietnam stretching from the Demilitarized Zone in the north to Sa Huynh at the boundary of Military Region 2 to the south. Most of the area was made up of jungles and mountains of the Truong Son range which sloped down from high peaks along the Laotian border toward the sea. Between the piedmont area of this mountain range and the coastline lay a narrow strip of cultivated land along which ran national Route QL-1. This was where most of the local population lived. The two northern provinces of MR-1, Quang Tri and Thua Thien where Hue was located, were separated from the three provinces to the south, Quang Nam, Quang Tin, and Quang Ngai, by an escarpment which projected into the sea at the Hai Van Pass. Da Nang, just south of this pass, was the biggest city of the region and the location of the Headquarters for ARVN I Corps. It was also a major port capable of accommodating sea-going vessels. A lesser port, Tan My, northeast of Hue, served as a military transportation terminal for shallow-draft vessels supplying ARVN units in northern MR-1. It was in this area that several major battles of the 1972 Easter invasion were fought.

The proximity to North Vietnam of MR-1 made it a major objective area which bore the brunt of constant heavy enemy pressure. For this reason Military Region 1 had earned the metaphorical name of "The Blazing Frontline." The rugged terrain definitely favored the enemy who also enjoyed the shortest supply lines from North Vietnam. Despite the enemy's advantages, and against great odds, MR-1 had always held firmly and bravely defended its territory, especially the Quang Tri front and the ancient capital city of Hue which was politically and psychologically important to both sides. For the defense of this area, ARVN forces in the two northern provinces, Quang Tri and Thua Thien, had at one time been reinforced with as many as five divisions -- three U.S. and the equivalent of two ARVN. This occurred when a major effort was made to recapture Hue during the 1968 Tet general offensive. Since then MR-1 had been dotted with a system of mutually supporting firebases and strongpoints, the more important ones were those located immediately south of the DMZ and west of Hue. *(Map 2)*

By March 1972, almost all U.S. combat units had redeployed from MR-1. The single remaining unit, the 196th Infantry Brigade, was standing down and conducted only defensive operations around Da Nang and Phu Bai airbases, pending return to the United States. Ground combat responsibilities were entirely assumed by ARVN units with the support of U.S. tactical air and naval gunfire and the assistance of American advisers. In the area north of the Hai Van Pass, where 80,000 American troops had at one time been deployed, there were now only two ARVN infantry divisions supported by a number of newly-activated armor and artillery units. Total troop strength committed to the defense of this area did not exceed 25,000.

The backbone of I Corps forces which were responsible for the defense of MR-1 consisted of three ARVN infantry divisions, the 1st, 2d and 3d, the 51st Infantry Regiment, the 1st Ranger Group (with 3 mobile and 6 border defense battalions) and the 1st Armor Brigade. Other combat forces organic to I Corps included the 10th Combat Engineer Group and corps artillery units. The territorial forces of MR-1, whose key combat components were the six Regional Forces (RF) battalions and company groups, also contributed significantly to area security in all five provinces. I Corps, commanded by Lieutenant General Hoang Xuan Lam, exercised control over all regular and territorial forces assigned to MR-1. General Lam, an armor officer, was a native of Hue.[1]

---

[1] Hue was the capital city of Central Vietnam, an ancient state whose dominions had extended from Thanh Hoa Province, now in North Vietnam, to Phan Rang; generally the coastal areas of GVN MR's 1 and 2.

Map 2 — Key Locations and Fire Support Bases, MR-1

On the eve of the enemy offensive, the general disposition of I Corps forces saw the 3d Infantry Division, which was activated six months earlier, assigned to secure the northernmost frontiers of South Vietnam. Although the division had never fought a coordinated battle as a division, its battalions were seasoned combat teams with long experience fighting in northern Quang Tri. Most of the 3d Division soldiers were natives of the region, familiar with its terrain and hardened to the harsh, cold dampness of its weather. The battalions of the 56th and 57th Regiments, in particular, were veterans of the DMZ. They occupied base camps and strongpoints they had been in for years and their dependents lived in the nearby hamlets. Considering the time and expense that would have been involved, it would not have been practical to even consider replacing the 3d Division on the DMZ front with another division, simply to gain the advantages that might ensue because of more experience in division-level operations.[2] The plain fact was that the battalions of the 3d Division were the most experienced in the DMZ area of any in the ARVN and they were expected to perform better than any others in that environment.

The 3d Division was generally responsible for the province of Quang Tri. Its headquarters, under the command of Brigadier General Vu Van Giai, former deputy commander of the 1st Division, was located at Quang Tri Combat Base. Two of the division's three regiments, the newly activated 56th and 57th, were deployed over a series of strongpoints and fire support bases dotting the area immediately south of the DMZ from the coastline to the piedmont area in the west. The 56th Regiment was headquartered at Fire Support Base (FSB) Carroll while the 57th Regiment was located at FSB C1. The 2d Regiment, which was formerly a component of the 1st Division, occupied Camp Carroll with two of its battalions at FSB C2. Camp Carroll was a large combat base

---

[2]Making a permanent shift in deployment of an ARVN division was a major undertaking, since it involved relocating thousands of families as well as soldiers and equipment. It took seven months to complete the move of the ARVN 25th Division from Quang Ngai to Hau Nghia.

situated 7 km southwest of the district town of Cam Lo on Route QL-9 which was the main road leading west to the Laotian border. The 11th Armored Cavalry Squadron, organic to the division, was located near Landing Zone (LZ) Sharon. The key firebases which supported the 3d Division were: C1, C2, and Camp Carroll.

In addition to its organic units, the 3d Division exercised operational control over two marine brigades of the general reserve, the 147th and 258th, which were deployed over an arched ridge line overlooking Route QL-9 to the west and the Thach Han River to the south. The 147th Marine Brigade was headquartered at Mai Loc Combat Base while its sister, the 258th Brigade was at FSB Nancy. These marine dispositions formed a strong line of defense facing west, the direction of most probably enemy attacks, and provided protection for the population in the lowlands of Quang Tri. Under the supervision of the 3d Division, but not directly controlled by it, were the regional force elements which manned a line of outposts facing the DMZ from Route QL-1 to the coastline. These elements were under the command of Quang Tri Sector and Gio Linh Subsector.

South of the Quang Tri - Thua Thien provincial boundary and north of the Hai Van Pass, lay the tactical area of responsibility (TAOR) of the 1st Infantry Division commanded by Major General Pham Van Phu. Its primary mission was to defend the western approaches to Hue. It deployed the 1st Regiment at Camp Evans, the 3d Regiment at FSB T-Bone and the 54th Regiment at FSB Bastogne. The division headquarters was located at Camp Eagle, just south of Hue. The 7th Armored Cavalry Squadron, organic to the 1st Division, was located with the 1st Infantry Regiment at Camp Evans.

The three provinces of southern MR-1, all located south of Hai Van Pass, were the responsibility of the 2d Infantry Division, commanded by Brigadier General Phan Hoa Hiep. The division headquarters was at Chu Lai in Quang Tin Province where the 4th Armored Cavalry, organic to the division, was also located. Each of the division's three regiments was assigned to a separate province. The 5th Regiment operated near Hoi An in Quang Nam Province; the 6th Regiment was headquartered at FSB Artillery Hill in Quang Tin Province, and the 4th Regiment at FSB Bronco in Quang Ngai Province. In view of its large territorial responsibilities, the 2d Division was assisted by six ranger border defense battalions.

Among I Corps forces, the 1st Armor Brigade -- which was to play an important role in the battle for Quang Tri -- had not been involved in actual combat for more than a year. The brigade's last combat action took place during the LAM SON 719 operation in lower Laos from February to April, 1971 where it had suffered high combat losses. Despite extensive reorganization and refitting efforts, which included the activation of the 20th Tank Squadron, our only unit equipped with M-48 medium tanks, the combat worthiness of the 1st Armor Brigade was still untested and difficult to evaluate.

While the 1st and 2d Infantry Divisions were thoroughly combat proven, the 3d Infantry Division was just organized as a unit on 1 October 1971. Two of its three regiments, the 56th and 57th, had been formed and deployed in forward positions along the DMZ barely three weeks before the invasion took place. At that time, the division did not have its own logistic support units and its artillery was still receiving equipment. But the overall status of the division seemed to be fairly good, the morale of its troops was high, and its unit training programs were on schedule. The division commander was professionally capable and highly dedicated to his job; his leadership inspired confidence among subordinate units. The division was still short of many critical items, especially signal communications. Despite this, the division endeavored to develop its combat capabilities through uninterrupted training which appeared to be quite effective. However, in no way could have the 3d Division be considered as fully prepared to fight a large, conventional action.

The two marine brigades which were placed under the operational control of the 3d Division were in every respect thoroughly combat effective. They were both at full strength, well equipped and well supplied through their own channels. But while their reputation as elite units of the RVNAF was solid and their combat valor held in high esteem, they were seldom totally responsive to the directives and requirements of the 3d Division commander. It was an unfortunate fact of life in the RVNAF that the loyalties of marine corps units belonged first to the marine corps commander and only second to the commander of the division or corps to which they were attached or assigned. This idiosyncracy was illustrated, and caused some serious tactical problems, during the LAM SON 719 operation into Laos in 1971. The reasons for this attitude were deep-seated and founded in the fact the ARVN infantry divisions had very little experience in multi-battalion operations, their commanders and staffs had little training and less interest in assuming the responsibilities that come with attachments, and attached units had to rely upon their parent organizations for all kinds of support. Furthermore, attached units, whether they were airborne, marine, ranger or armor often found themselves shunted off to the side, or sent on poorly planned and imperfectly executed operations.

As far as I Corps Headquarters was concerned, it had never really directed and controlled large, coordinated combat operations except for the unique case of LAM SON 719 during which it operated as a command post in the field for the first time. Although the I Corps staff excelled in procedural and administrative work and was effective in the operation and control of routine territorial security activities, it lacked the experience, professionalism and initiative required of a field staff during critical times during battle.

During the month of January 1972, orders were issued by I Corps to all major subordinate units, alerting them to be prepared for a big enemy offensive during the Tet holidays. This was done merely to comply with orders from Saigon since the I Corps commander saw nothing to indicate an iminent major enemy offensive. Although Saigon had concluded that the preparation for movement and combat that had been detected among the NVA divisions north of the DMZ were reason enough to alert the command, these divisions were still far from the line of contact and General Lam saw no cause for immediate alarm. He took cognizance of the enemy's logistical build-up in the area north and west of the I Corps defenses, but still he believed that the Communist Tet actions

would be limited to an increase in shellings and sapper attacks on
RVNAF lines of communications. General Lam would reserve his concern
for the time when the NVA divisions moved into staging areas on the
western flank of Quang Tri Province, in western Thua Thien, and southern
MR-1. Indications of these deployments were always seen prior to
previous offensives and they were, so far, absent.

And so, appropriate measures were taken by I Corps forces to
counteract the enemy's harassment activities rather than fully brace
themselves for a major enemy offensive. ARVN units indeed reacted
effectively to enemy-initiated activities throughout MR-1, and the Tet
holidays passed in relative calm. Intelligence officers and tactical
commanders, meanwhile, closely monitored and waited for signs of
movement of NVA forces. Their correct prediction of the enemy's scope
of activities for the Tet period reinforced their confidence that he
would probably not depart from his established pattern of making
deliberate deployments, which would be detected, prior to launching
the offensive.

By February, this assessment of the situation gained further
credibility when it was revealed that the NVA 324B Division was moving
into the A Shau Valley in western Thua Thien Province. This was a
familiar and often used staging area for this enemy division to launch
attacks against Hue. The 1st ARVN Infantry Division deployed accordingly
to preempt this move and clashed violently with NVA units along Route 547
west of Hue in early March. What remained to be confirmed as definite
indications of the predicted offensive in MR-1 was the movement of elements
of the NVA 304th and 308th Divisions into western Quang Tri Province.
While there were unconfirmed reports that the 66th Regiment of the 304th
Division was in the Ba Long Valley near FSB Sarge, the location of the
other two regiments, the 9th and 24th, were unknown at that time. They
were believed to be just north of the DMZ as was the entire 308th Division.

General Lam did not believe in the theory that the NVA might
attack across the DMZ although the danger of such an attack had not
been ruled out; this had never happened before. This no-man's land
was mostly flat, exposed terrain, unfavorable for the maneuver of large

22

infantry formations, even with armor support, since they would be under observation and fire from our powerful tactical air, artillery and armored forces in addition to our system of solid strongpoints. Additional indications of NVA troop movements into western Quang Tri Province also reinforced his belief that if the enemy was to strike, he would probably come from the west, his usual avenue of approach. Indeed, enemy efforts to open new roads and bring in more anti-aircraft weapons in this area made General Lam's assessment even more convincing. But the offensive was not imminent, he reasoned, since enemy preparations were taking place at an apparently slow pace.

When confronted with the possibility of a NVA drive across the DMZ, General Giai, commander of the 3d Division, had the same reaction as General Lam. He, too, believed that any large attack would come from the west although he did not reject completely the possibility of an attack from the north since he knew there were indications that the enemy had brought surface-to-air (SAM) missiles, additional 130-mm field guns, ammunition and armor in the area just north of the DMZ, and beginning on 27 March there was a marked increase in indirect fire attacks against the division's fire support bases in the DMZ area. But General Giai was facing more pressing problems in his area of operation (AO) at that time. His primary concern was to consolidate his recently occupied defensive positions to the west, train and continue to prepare his division for the enemy offensive. Nevertheless, he and his staff were continually debating the problem of dominant terrain features, the enemy's most probable course of action, the disposition of his units, the configuration of their defense positions and above all, how to employ his forces effectively in the event of an enemy offensive.

While his staff was developing comprehensive plans for the defense of the division's area of responsibility, General Giai initiated a program of rotating his units among the regimental areas of operation in order to familiarize them thoroughly with the terrain and to eliminate the "firebase syndrome" among his troops. In accordance with this program, on 30 March the 56th and 57th Regiments began the scheduled exchange of their AO's. The 56th Regiment was to take over the 2d Regiment's AO to include Camp Carroll, FSB Khe Gio and FSB Fuller; it would be responsible for the northwest defense line. The 57th Regiment was moving into the 56th's AO which extended from Dong Ha due north to the DMZ and east to the coastline. The 2d Regiment, meanwhile, was taking over the combat bases north of Cam Lo in the AO just vacated by the 56th. By midday, this exchange of AOs had been about half-completed when the enemy struck in force.

During the month preceding the offensive, the 1st Infantry Division to the south had been aggressively operating in the areas west and southwest of Hue where it cleared the approaches to FSBs Rakkasan and Bastogne in preparation for future operations towards the A Shau Valley. A major enemy buildup was evidently in progress in this area, but the division's initiatives preempted attacks against FSB Bastogne. Enemy elements positively identified were the MR Tri-Thien - Hue's 6th Regiment and the 803th and 29th Regiments of the NVA 342B Division. Resistance by these enemy units was strong and they appeared determined to control the area around FSB Veghel, the Cu Mong Grotto and Route 547 despite the effective attacks conducted by the 1st Division.

The Initial Battles

The enemy offensive began at noon on 30 March with artillery concentrations directed against strongpoints and firebases of the 3d Division. This fire was well-planned and accurate. It was easy for the enemy to determine the exact locations and dispositions of ARVN troops since these positions had been used by both U.S. and ARVN forces for many years. Additionally, the enemy's long-range 130-mm field guns just north of the DMZ had the key ARVN positions in this area well within their fields of fire. These deadly concentrations pounded Camp Carroll, Mai Loc, Sarge, Holcomb, A4, A2, C1, C2 and Dong Ha Combat Base while elements of the 56th and 57th Regiments were still displacing toward their new locations, FSBs Carroll and Charlie 1 respectively.

These artillery fires were followed by and coordinated with ground attacks, spearheaded by tanks, and came from the north across the DMZ and from the west through Khe Sanh. *(Map 3)* From the north, the enemy push consisted of four spearheads. Two of them were directed against positions of the 56th Regiment in the vicinity of FSB Fuller and FSB A4. The other two moved along and parallel to Route QL-1 and were directed against the 57th Regiment's positions at FSB A2 and FSB A1. Meanwhile, from the west, the NVA drive was directed against the 147th Marine Brigade at Nui Ba Ho, FSB Sarge and FSB Holcomb. As confirmed later, enemy forces conducting these initial attacks included elements of the NVA 304th and 308th Divisions, three separate infantry regiments of the B-5 Front, two armor regiments, five artillery regiments and at least one sapper battalion.

The unexpected assault across the DMZ caught the forward elements of the 3d Division in movement, only partially settled into defensive positions they had not been in for some time, locally outnumbered three-to-one, and out-gunned by the enemy artillery. The ARVN defenses in the DMZ area were designed to counter infiltration and local attacks. There were no positions prepared to give the depth to the battlefield that would be required to contain an attack of the size and momentum of the one that had now fallen upon them.

Enemy attacks increased in intensity during the next day. All firebases along the perimeter of the 3d Division received heavy artillery fire. The 56th, 57th and 2d Regiments and the marine battalions were all in contact with attacking forces. Nui Ba Ho was evacuated late in the evening and Sarge was overrun during the early hours of 1 April, forcing the marines to fall back to Mai Loc. Enemy pressure forced elements of the 56th Regiment near FSB Fuller and those of the 2d Regiment near Khe Gio to withdraw south of the Cam Lo River. By evening of 1 April, all strongpoints along the northern perimeter had been evacuated, including FSB Fuller and FSB Khe Gio. The withdrawal from A1, A4, and other strongpoints, including those manned by RF troops, was orderly and executed in accordance with plans and consistent with the tactical situation. However, serious mistakes were committed

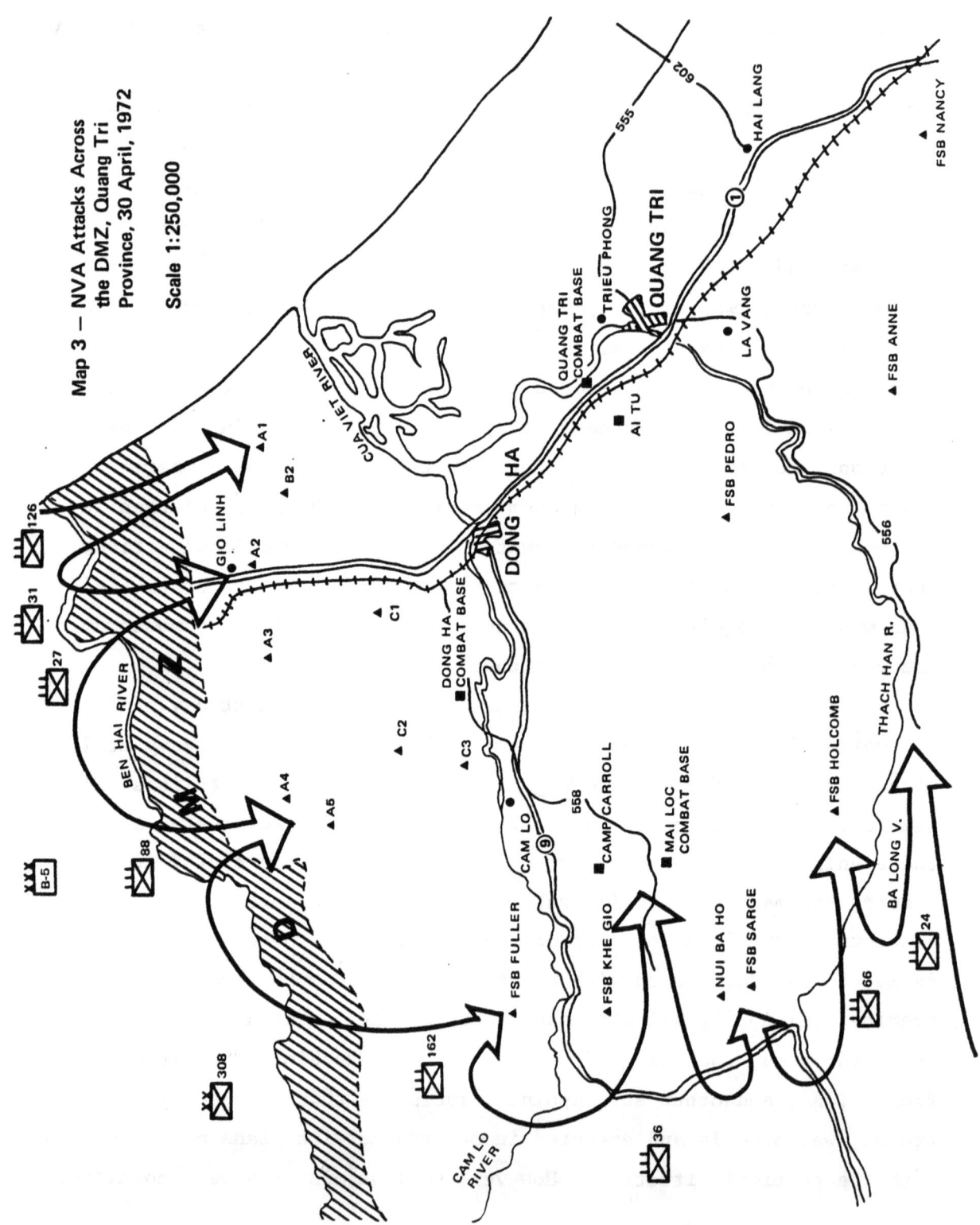

at A2 and C1 where two artillery batteries were located. The failure of these two bases to obtain prime movers forced the destruction and abandonment of 12 artillery pieces (six 105-mm and six 155-mm howitzers). By this time, the 56th Regiment had withdrawn to Camp Carroll and was under attack. The 57th Regiment had fallen back to north of Dong Ha and the 2d Regiment to Cam Lo. The marine units, meanwhile remained at Mai Loc and FSB Pedro. As a result of intense enemy artillery fire on Quang Tri Combat Base, the 3d Division Headquarters was relocated to the citadel in Quang Tri City.

At 1800 hours on 1 April, General Giai ordered an immediate reorganization of defensive positions. His concept was to take advantage of natural obstacles such as the Cua Viet and Mieu Giang Rivers and establish a line of defense south of these rivers. All divisional forces north of Dong Ha were ordered to withdraw south. The RF and PF units were to hold a line on the southern bank of the Cua Viet River from the coastline to approximately 5 kilometers inland; the 57th Regiment would establish its positions westward from that point to Dong Ha. The city and its immediate vicinity were placed under control of the 1st Armor Brigade whose major component, the 20th Tank Squadron, had been hastily thrown into combat as it was about to complete training at Camp Evans. West from Dong Ha and south of the Mieu Giang River, the 2d Regiment was given responsibility for a line at Cam Lo, reinforced with an armored cavalry squadron. Next to the 2d Regiment was the 56th, reinforced with the 11th Armored Cavalry Squadron which was ordered to hold Camp Carroll. This defensive line then extended southward to join the 147th Marine Brigade's AO around Mai Loc. Marine battalions were also ordered to occupy the high ground along Route QL-9 between Cam Lo and Mai Loc, secure Quang Tri Combat Base and continue operations near FSB Pedro. *(Map 4)*

The 3d Division's defense on 2 April appeared to be well-organized. The disposition of divisional forces was good and the division headquarters had fairly tight control over its subordinate units. General Giai personally supervised the division's organization for defense and his conspicious presence at some forward positions restored and

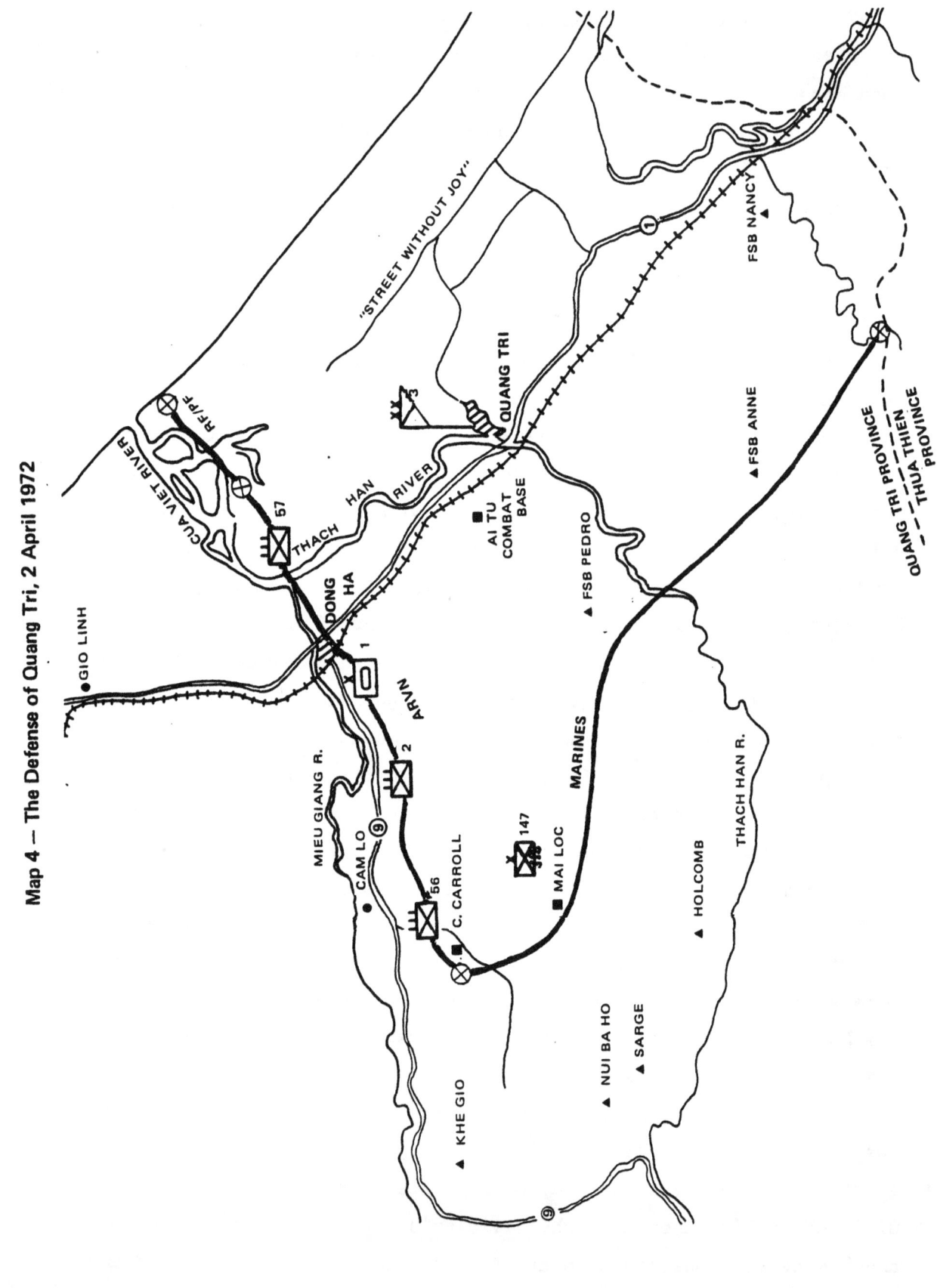

Map 4 — The Defense of Quang Tri, 2 April 1972

greatly stimulated morale and self-assurance among his troops. During the following days, the forces that manned the Cua Viet River line -- the 57th Regiment, the 1st Armored Brigade and particularly the RF and PF -- fully demonstrated their combat capabilities and were all up to their assigned tasks. They repeatedly repelled the enemy's attempts to cross the river and inflicted heavy losses. The new 20th Tank Squadron also proved effective in its confrontation with NVA tanks, preventing them from approaching river-crossing points at Dong Ha. To the west and southwest, the marines held firmly their positions at the two major bases, Mai Loc and Pedro. They seemed unaffected by their initial setbacks at Sarge, Nui Ba Ho and Holcomb.

The day of 2 April was marked by several tragic events. It began with simultaneous enemy attacks against Dong Ha and Camp Carroll. Again, bad weather precluded effective use of tactical air throughout most of the day. From morning to late evening, enemy tanks and infantry forces repeatedly tried to approach Dong Ha from the north. They were engaged by our 57th Regiment, the 20th Tank Squadron, the 3d Marine Battalion, U.S. Naval gunfire and were repulsed at every attempt to cross the Dong Ha bridge. The chaotic stream of refugees fleeing the combat scene along Route QL-1 since early morning deeply affected the morale of the 57th Regiment's troops who broke ranks around noon and withdrew south in disorder. If there had been a plan to evacuate civilians from the battle area, and if that plan had been well executed with suitable control and transportation, the troops of the 57th would have probably remained on position. But when they saw the disorder and panic among these refugees -- among whom were their own families and relatives -- the panic was contagious. When General Giai received word of what was happening, he immediately flew to the position. His presence there restored the confidence of the soldiers and they returned to their units. To stall the enemy's armor-infantry drive, the Dong Ha bridge was destroyed by ARVN engineers at 1630 hours.

Camp Carroll to the west, in the meantime, had been surrounded by enemy troops since early morning. Troops of the 56th Regiment at the camp valiantly endured heavy artillery fires and resisted repeated assaults by enemy infantry but received little effective artillery or air support since fire support coordination was poorly planned. The regimental commander, Colonel Pham Van Dinh, who had often proven his courage and devotion (he was the officer who restored the national colors at the Hue Citadel during the 1968 offensive) was despondent. The division was giving him no support and the corps seemed to have forgotten about him. Seeing that his situation was hopeless and wanting to save as many of his soldiers lives as possible, he called his staff together and announced that he would surrender the command. He ordered his S-2 to carry a white sheet to the main gate of the compound and hang it there. This done, radio contact was made with the enemy and arrangements for the surrender were made. Fifteen hundred ARVN troops were captured along with 22 artillery pieces, including a 175-mm battery and numerous quad-50's and twin-40's, the largest artillery assemblage in the entire MR-1. The 56th Regiment no longer existed.

The loss of Camp Carroll made the defense of Mai Loc nearby extremely precarious. The 147th Marine Brigade commander decided that this base could not be held and upon his request, General Giai authorized its evacuation. The marines fell back to Quang Tri late in the afternoon. And so, repeatedly over the last three days these marine elements had been forced to withdraw and the 3d Division's AO was shrinking accordingly from both directions, the north and the west. These withdrawals had been orderly but the brigade had suffered such heavy losses during the battles of the first few days that immediately upon reaching Quang Tri it was ordered to proceed directly to Hue for regrouping and refitting. It was replaced by a fresh unit, the 369th Marine Brigade which immediately set up a new defense around FSB Nancy.

This rotation had a revitalizing effect on the marine troops in the combat zone. It proved to be a vital factor which contributed to the maintenance of a high level of marine combat effectiveness throughout the enemy offensive. Unfortunately for the ARVN troops of the 3d Infantry Division, the 1st Armor Brigade, and the ranger groups which came as reinforcement, rotation seldom occurred.

Holding the Line

After four days of arduous fighting and tragic setbacks, the friendly situation on the Quang Tri front remained critical. However, there were high hopes that the new defense line would stand firmly. Despite severe blows, both ARVN regular and territorial forces seemed to hold extremely well along this new line. To their credit, they had stopped the NVA invasion -- for the time being. They had performed their task well, not through reliance on U.S. air support but with their own combat support. In fact, prolonged bad weather continued to preclude effective tactical air support and severely curtailed the use of helicopter gunships. But U.S. naval gunfire was helpful; so were B-52 strikes which were conducted five or six times a day against suspected NVA troop concentrations and avenues of approach.

The loss of Camp Carroll and Mai Loc resulted in heavy personnel and materiel sacrifices and had an adverse psychological impact on South Vietnam, but did not seem to dampen either the morale or the self-assurance of the defending forces. In the week that followed, the feeling of self-assurance among ARVN troops on the firing line increased. Every attempt by the enemy to break through was thoroughly defeated. According to unit reports, several enemy attacking formations were broken up, scattered and forced to withdraw in utter disorder under the shattering fire of our infantry, armor and artillery.

The enemy now withdrew to regroup and only scattered contacts and attacks by fire occurred throughout the 3d Division's area of responsibility. Although the weather continued to prevent the full use of U.S. tactical air support, the ARVN defense line held.

In the meantime, three ARVN ranger groups, the 1st, 4th and 5th, arrived to reinforce the defense of Quang Tri. As the weather showed some signs of improving, the I Corps commander gave serious consideration to a counterattack which was to be launched as soon as tactical air could apply its full weight. His preoccupation with plans for a counterattack diverted the I Corps staff from reorganizing the defense in depth, an effort that should have been first priority under the circumstances. This failure to recognize this proved to be a serious error that subsequently led to the loss of Quang Tri City.

Apparently, General Lam was overly influenced by the arrival of reinforcements. First to arrive was the 369th Marine Brigade, followed by the Ranger Command with the three groups of three battalions each, all freshly arrived from Saigon. General Lam believed that with these additional forces he could not only hold the two northern provinces but also retake the lost territory in a short time.

With this conviction, General Lam repeatedly rejected the 3d Division commander's requests for reinforcement to consolidate the defense of Quang Tri. But General Giai was insistent and finally the I Corps commander reluctantly sent him first one ranger group, then another. Eventually, all four ranger groups in MR-1 were deployed to Quang Tri and attached to the 3d Division. The attachments were intended to provide General Giai with full operational control and unity of command.

However, despite its growing span of control, the 3d Division never received additional support in logistics and signal communications essential for the effective exercise of command and control. This problem was recognized at the time by the I Corps staff which recommended that the control burden placed on General Giai should be reduced. This could have been accomplished by placing the Marine Division under the command of I Corps, and by giving the Marine Division and the Ranger Command each the responsibility for a separate sector. But for reasons known only to General Lam, these recommendations were brushed aside. Perhaps General Lam did not feel certain he could handle the Marine Division commander who, during LAM SON 719, had failed to comply with his orders but still came out unscathed. As a result the Headquarters, Ranger Command, under Colonel Tran Cong Lieu, was left in Da Nang without a specific assignment while the Marine Division Headquarters in Hue was not under I Corps command. This state of things provided additional problems for the 3d Division commander who frequently found that the orders he gave to his attached units had no effect until the subordinate commander had checked and received guidance from his parent headquarters. This was especially true if the orders required a difficult operation.

But General Lam seemed oblivious to the 3d Division commander's problems. His mood was optimistic. He believed that I Corps had enough forces to stop NVA units at the present line of defense while he and his staff were working on a plan to launch a counteroffensive.

General Lam's optimism was justified by the events of 9 April. On that day, the enemy launched a second major effort, again from the north and the west. But once again, the defense succeeded in driving back all attacks. The 1st Armor Brigade, the 258th Marine Brigade and the 5th Ranger Group all reported success. Several enemy tanks were knocked out by the marines using LAW rockets and by the tank guns of the 1st Armor Brigade. FSB Pedro, which had been overrun that day was retaken the next day after 3d Division troops had repulsed three major attacks. Once more, the enemy had failed to break through the ARVN line of defense even though he had thrown into his effort major elements of the 304th and 308th NVA Divisions and two armor reigments. At the end of the day, the 3d Division's perimeter, which ran from the coastline along the Cua Viet River westward through Dong Ha then veered south to join FSB Pedro and the Thach Han River, was still intact.

By this time, General Giai's personal responsibilities and span of control had expanded far beyond that normally expected for a division commander. As a division commander, he found himself exercising command over two infantry regiments of his own, operational control over two marine brigades, four ranger groups, one armor brigade plus all the territorial forces of Quang Tri Province. The 3d Division commander's span of control thus included nine brigades containing a total of twenty-three battalions, in addition to the territorial forces. His responsibilities also included supervising and providing protection for I Corps artillery and logistic units operating at Dong Ha, as well as monitoring the status of the provincial and district governments in Quang Tri. He was pleased and stimulated by the total trust the I Corps commander had vested in him.

Strange as it may seem, General Lam seldom felt the urge to visit

3d Division Soldier Digging In Near Dong Ha, 10 April 1972

A M-48 Tank of the 1st Armor Brigade Guarding Route QL-9 Near Cam Lo

his subordinate commanders in the field or the I Corps frontline units. He monitored the progress of battles through reports and he issued directives and orders from his headquarters. He never personally observed the 3d Division line of defense to determine the problems being faced by unit commanders. Apparently, he did not think the situation serious enough to warrant his presence. ARVN success during 9 and 10 April buoyed his optimism even more and led to his conviction that the time had arrived for a counterattack. As conceived by his staff, the plan called for an attack across the Cua Viet River in order to retake the district of Gio Linh and the entire area north to the DMZ. He was convinced that such an attack was within I Corps capabilities and would halt North Vietnam's invasion. If it succeeded, his counterattack might well force the enemy to withdraw all forces north of the DMZ.

Although the counterattack plan was thoroughly discussed and considered, it was finally discarded. For one thing, the amount of forces required for success in the northward drive would greatly weaken the western flank of the defense where the enemy was stronger. If the western flank should fail to remain intact, then Quang Tri City would be in serious jeopardy. Therefore, General Lam, after considerable deliberation, decided that the counteroffensive effort should be directed westward instead of to the north. He planned to re-establish the former line of defense in the west by launching an all-out attack to regain, phase line by phase line, such bases as Cam Lo, Camp Carroll and Mai Loc. At the same time, he ordered participating units to clear all enemy elements from their zones of advance before moving on to the next phase line. The counteroffensive was called Operation QUANG TRUNG 729, in an allusion to the same historical event the Communists exploited in naming their offensive. The imperial name of Nguyen Hue was Quang Trung; the operation was scheduled to begin on 14 April.

General Giai issued the orders to the 3d Division and its attached units and QUANG TRUNG 729 began. There was no great surge of infantry and armor crossing the line of departure, however. On the contrary, the weary troops on the western flank were already in close contact with the enemy, as they had been for two weeks, and were unwilling or unable to advance. NVA artillery fire was devastating and attrition in the ARVN ranks was heavy. By the end of the first week of the operation, no unit had advanced more than 500 meters from the line of departure. With his limited command and control facilities, General Giai found it impossible to coordinate a strong, well-supported attack in any part of the zone. Furthermore, it seemed that by this time he was not aware of the deteriorating state of morale among his subordinate commanders and their troops. These commanders had lost confidence in their ability to carry the attack to the enemy and, because General Giai was unable to exercise personal command over so many dispersed units, his subordinates were able to delay preparations for the attack by claiming logistic problems, personnel attrition, troop fatigue and every other possible reason to procrastinate. Although they sent General Giai daily reports of their attemps to advance, the line of contact remained unchanged. The orders they had to clear the zone of all enemy before advancing to the next phase line required a cautious, slow moving attack in any case, and provided them with ample justification for their inability to move faster.

Along with the reports General Giai received from his commanders describing their efforts to clear the enemy from their zones, came many requests for airstrikes against enemy concentrations, strikes that were necessary to soften the enemy before the ARVN battalions could begin the advance to the west. As the days wore on, the battalions in contact also flooded 3d Division headquarters with reports of heavy enemy attacks-by-fire and high friendly casualties. QUANG TRUNG 729 did not resemble an offensive, but rather had settled into a costly battle of attrition in place in which the ARVN battalions were steadily reduced in strength and effectiveness by the enemy's deadly artillery fire. Morale continued to deteriorate and General Giai was unable to restore it; neither was he able to prod his battalions out of their holes and bunkers and into the attack. It seemed that the subordinate commanders knew that their units lacked the strength to break through the NVA formations facing them, that the enemy's artillery would surely catch them in the open and destroy them, and that the coordinated fire and logistical support they would need to carry the attack was beyond the capability of the 3d Division or I Corps to provide.

It was during this time that the failure of I Corps to establish an effective command and control system became a serious problem. The Marine Division Headquarters and the Ranger Command, which had been sent to I Corps expressly to provide control over their organic units, continued to be left out of combat activities and received no specific assignments or responsibilities. But as parent headquarters of the marines and rangers committed to the combat zone, they contributed much to the confusion of command and control by elaborating on General Giai's orders or by questioning and commenting on everything concerning their units. They were not the only ones to do his, however. General Lam himself frequently issued directives by telephone or radio to individual brigade commanders, especially to the 1st Armor Brigade commander (who belonged to the same branch) and who rarely bothered to inform General Giai about these calls. General Giai often learned of these directives only after they had been implemented and these incidents seriously degraded his authority. Distrust and insubordination gradually set in and finally resulted in total disruption of command and control at the front line in northern MR-1.

After two weeks of continuous rain and heavy cloud cover, which seriously impeded the use of tactical air support, the weather began to improve. With an accelerated tempo as if to make up for time lost, U.S. aircraft of all types daily swarmed in the skies over Quang Tri. Air sorties by B-52's, tactical aircraft, gunships, increased steadily each day striking all suspicious targets. This upsurge restored the morale and self-assurance of the ground troops.

On 18 April, enemy activity increased substantially with attacks-by-fire and infantry-armor probes. This became the enemy's third major effort to take Quang Tri. All ARVN and marine units reported contact and indirect fire. At 1830 hours, a coordinated enemy attack was launched against the western sector of the 3d Division. From all positions, units reported movements of enemy tanks. Within the space of three hours, the U.S. Air Force responded with tactical air and B-52 missions diverted from elsewhere with such devastating strikes that the enemy attack was completely disrupted. This provided ARVN units with an opportunity to pass to the offensive and fully initiate the counteroffensive, QUANG TRUNG 729. But nothing happened; at daybreak, the troops still clung to their trenches and made no significant effort to move forward.

The fact that another major effort by the enemy had been effectively stopped deluded the I Corps commander into thinking once more that the situation in Quang Tri was under control. But the inertia developing among ARVN units should have alerted him to the pressing requirement for reorganizing his positions and rotating weary combat units. This need totally escaped him. The enemy's demonstrated ability to conduct a sustained offensive on the other hand should also have stimulated a major ARVN effort to implement a coordinated defense plan if Quang Tri was to be held. But this effort was not made.

The following week saw the defense line at Dong Ha and along the Cua Viet River cave in because of a tactical blunder. This came about when reports were received that the enemy was infiltrating from the west and threatening to cut off the supply route between Dong Ha and Quang Tri Combat Base. On his own initiative, the 1st Armor Brigade commander directed his 20th Tank Squadron on the Cua Viet line to pull back south along Route QL-1 in order to clear the enemy elements there. As soon as they saw the tanks move south, ARVN troops were gripped with panic, broke ranks and streamed along. Before the 3d Division commander detected what was happening, many of his troops had already arrived at Quang Tri Combat Base and the Cua Viet defense, which was one of our strongest lines of defense from which the courageous ARVN troops had repeatedly repelled every enemy attack for nearly a month, had been abandoned. It was virtually handed to the enemy on a platter because a tactical commander had taken it upon himself to initiate a major move without reporting to his superior and without foreseeing the consequences of his actions.

Once again, by sheer physical intercession, the 3d Division

commander succeeded in reestablishing order, although not for long. Much precious time had been lost. By the time he had finally regained control of the situation, there was no way to push his units back to Cua Viet to restore the lost positions. He was compelled to regroup them west of Quang Tri City and develop a new defense line north of the Thach Han River. This new line surrounded and protected the Quang Tri Combat Base whose importance as a logistic support center had greatly diminished in view of the dwindling supplies still available there.

On 23 April, the 147th Marine Brigade returned to Quang Tri Base to take over its defense after a rest and refitting period in Hue. The 258th Marine Brigade redeployed to Hue but its 1st Battalion remained at FSB Pedro and came under operational control of the 147th.

During the days that followed, the morale of ARVN troops deteriorated rapidly. They were exposed to the daily poundings of enemy artillery and assaults by enemy tanks. They became vulnerable to the intense tempo of conventional warfare. They had to spend long nights, tense, sleepless, agonizing at the prospect of enemy infantry assaults which could surge forward from the dark at any moment. The near-total inertia of ARVN troops at night made it possible for the enemy to rest and recuperate at almost any time he chose. Therefore, short lulls during the fighting were invariably the time enemy troops chose to rest. ARVN troops in the meantime were constantly kept on the alert, under tension day and night, their energy sapped by fear and uncertainty while often defending a combat base of dubious tactical value.

Quang Tri Combat Base, north of the Thach Han River, was in fact a bad choice for defense from a tactical point of view. As the month of April was drawing to its end, so were the supplies at this base. Consequently, the 3d Division commander decided then to evacuate this base and withdraw south of the river. He worked on the withdrawal plan by himself; he consulted only the division senior adviser. General Giai feared that if his subordinate commanders learned of his plan, they were apt to wreck it through hasty actions. He also deliberately withheld this plan from the I Corps commander. He simply wanted to be cautious, to get things done. But it was this action that alienated him from the I Corps commander and the growing distrust that developed between them added a further dimension to the events which eventually led to the fall of Quang Tri City.

The Fall of Quang Tri City

The final NVA actions that contributed to the fall of Quang Tri City occurred during the last week of April. By this time, the effect of strain and shock from four weeks of conventional warfare on ill-prepared ARVN troops had taken its toll on unit discipline and effectiveness. Gone were the last remaining shreds of self-assurance and cohesiveness. Units of the 3d Division fought on without much conviction and were practically left to fend for themselves. The division's sector was shrinking with every passing day. *(Map 5)*

During this time enemy attacks from the west near the boundary of Thua Thien Province cut off Route QL-1 to the south and interdicted all friendly vehicular traffic over a seven kilometer stretch. This isolated I Corps forces in Quang Tri Province and completely severed the lifeline which sustained them in combat. The I Corps commander's first reaction to this situation was a series of directives to ARVN logistic units to push supply convoys through the enemy road blocks. Next, the 3d Division commander was repeatedly ordered to clear Route QL-1 from the north. These orders compelled General Giai to divert an armored cavalry squadron from its vital frontline role near Quang Tri to conduct operations to the south. Finally, the I Corps commander deployed a fresh marine battalion which was committed to the defense of Hue to clear Route QL-1 from the south. These movements severely exhausted fuel and ammunition supplies so critically needed in Quang Tri but were unsuccessful in reopening this vital lifeline.

The weather was particularly bad on 27 April and the enemy took advantage of it. Actions on that day signaled the beginning of the NVA push to capture all remaining territory held by ARVN troops in Quang Tri Province. Along the 3d Division's new defense line, which

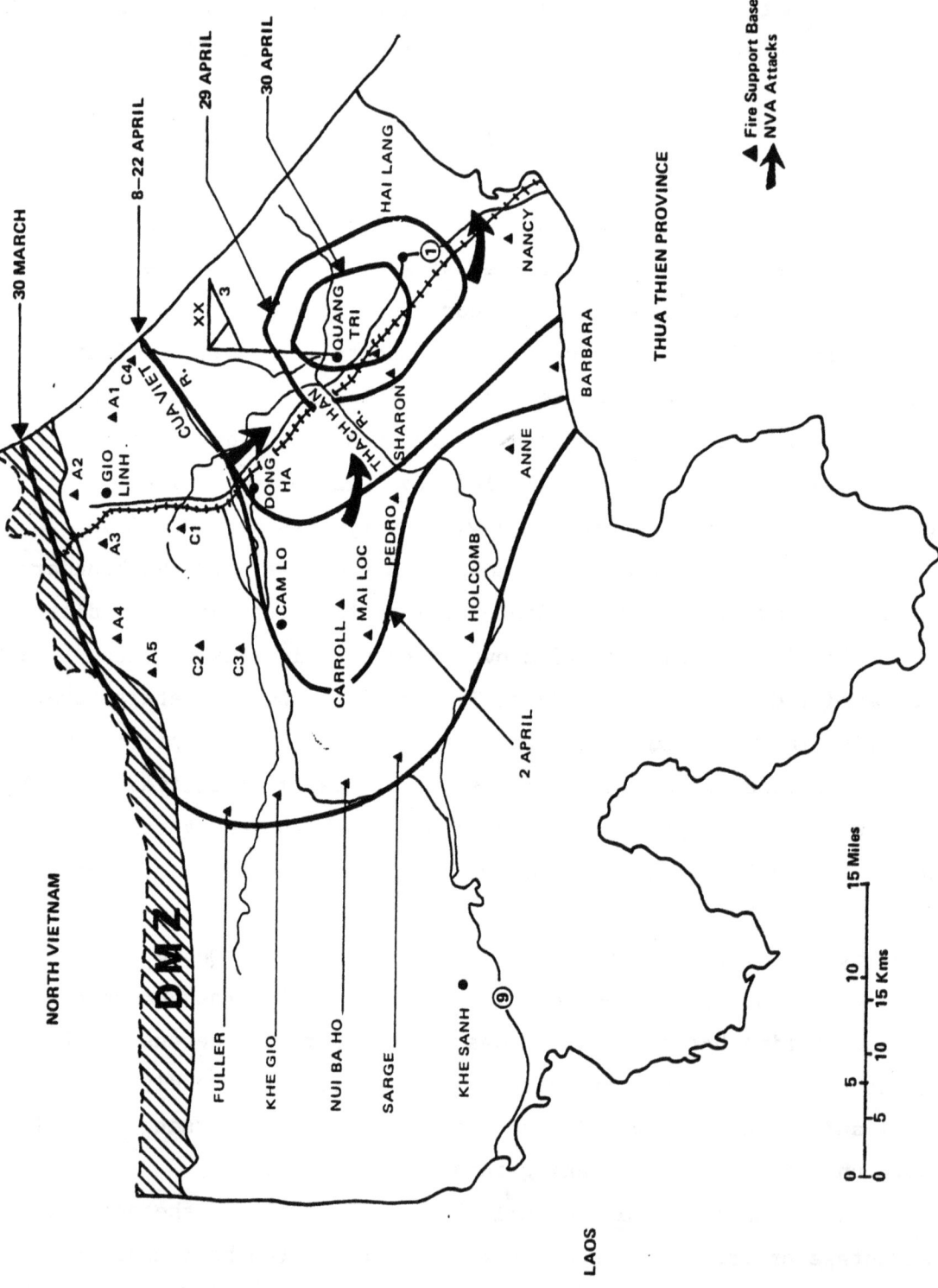

Map 5 — The Shrinking 3d Infantry Division AO, Quang Tri Province

had shrunk to the immediate vicinity of Quang Tri City to the east, north, and west, units either reported contact with enemy troops or received enemy artillery fire. Throughout the day all forward elements of the division were under fire and engaged by tank-supported enemy infantry. Most units lost some ground but were holding precariously. At the end of the day, most elements of the 1st Armor Brigade were pushed back to within two to three kilometers of Route QL-1 while enemy artillery fire concentrated heavily on the Quang Tri Combat Base. In response to the 3d Division commander's declared tactical emergency, U.S. tactical air and B-52 bombers braved adverse weather to stop the enemy advance on Quang Tri.

The next day, 28 April, enemy tanks approached the Quang Tri Bridge, about two kilometers southwest of Quang Tri City, which was the responsibility of the 2d Regiment. The armored cavalry squadron, which had been sent to reinforce the 2d Regiment was holding the bridge but it was forced to pull back. Elements of the 1st Armor Brigade also experienced setbacks during the day and had withdrawn to within one kilometer north of Quang Tri Combat Base. The brigade commander meanwhile had been wounded and evacuated. With his departure, discipline crumbled and the 1st Armor Brigade troops fled south along Route QL-1, passing through a road block set up by the 147th Marine Brigade.

The 57th Regiment in the meantime had become ineffective. Its commander had no knowledge of the status of his two battalions that had been near Dong Ha City. The only troops he had with him were those of a reconnaissance platoon. Throughout the night, men continued to flow south. The only effective unit still defending Quang Tri Combat Base was the 147th Marine Brigade and it was under heavy and continuous 130-mm gun fire.

By 29 April, the situation in Quang Tri Province had become critical. The enemy's renewed initiative pointed toward another major effort. On their part, ARVN unit commanders at this time were extremely concerned about fuel and ammunition shortages. Several howitzers had already been destroyed after all available ammunition was expended.

The ARVN effort to reopen Route QL-1 meanwhile progressed at a snail's pace for lack of coordination and positive effort; its outlook was not promising. Quang Tri was kept resupplied by helicopters which took extreme risks approaching the city, especially by way of Route QL-1.

In the face of this pending tactical disaster, on 30 April, General Giai summoned subordinate commanders to his headquarters and presented his plan to withdraw south of the Thach Han River. Basically, the plan consisted of holding Quang Tri City with a marine brigade, establishing a defense line on the southern bank of the Thach Han River with infantry and ranger troops and releasing enough tank and armored cavalry units for the pressing task of reopening Route QL-1 to the south. All units were to move during the morning of the next day, 1 May. Informed of General Giai's withdrawal plan, General Lam tacitly concurred although he never confirmed his approval. Neither did he issue any directives to the 3d Division commander.

In the morning of 1 May, however, General Lam called the 3d Division commander and said that he did not approve the withdrawal plan. He issued orders to General Giai to the effect that all units were to remain where they were and hold their positions "at all costs." He also made it clear to General Giai that no withdrawal of any unit would be permitted unless he personally gave the authorization. General Lam's eleventh-hour countermand turned out to be a reiteration of President Thieu's directive which had just been received from Saigon. This decision was being taken presumably because the Paris peace talks had just been resumed after being boycotted by the RVN delegation since the beginning of the NVA invasion.

It was easy to pick up the telephone and countermand an order. In the field and under heavy enemy pressure, these conflicting orders inevitably resulted in a nightmare of confusion and chaos. General Giai did not even have sufficient time to countermand his own orders and at the same time impart the new orders to each of his subordinates through a lengthy series of radio calls. Furthermore all brigade and regimental commanders were not in a position to carry out the new orders.

Some of them claimed that their units had already moved to new positions according to plan; others bluntly refused to change a course of action which had already been initiated. General Giai persisted in convincing them to comply with the new instructions received from I Corps. He reiterated the new orders and emphasized that each unit must comply. He also rescinded a previous order to relocate his command post and remained in Quang Tri City.

And so within the space of four hours, the ARVN dispositions for defense crumbled completely. Those units to the north manning positions around Quang Tri Combat Base streamed across the Thach Han River and continued their way south with the uncontainable force of a flood over broken dam. The mechanized elements that reached Quang Tri Bridge were unable to cross; the bridge had already been destroyed. They left behind all vehicles and equipment and forded the river toward the south. On the southern bank of the river, infantry units did not remain long in their new positions. As soon as they detected ARVN tanks withdrawing south, they deserted their positions and joined the column. But this column did not progress far. Tanks and armored vehicles began to run out of fuel and one by one they were left behind by their crews along Route QL-1. The only unit that retained full cohesiveness and control during this time was the 147th Marine Brigade which was defending Quang Tri City. Finally the brigade commander decided for himself that the situation was hopeless and he too ordered his unit to move out of Quang Tri at 1430 hours leaving behind the 3d Division commander and his skeletal staff all alone in the undefended city's old citadel.

Finally, when he learned what was happening, the 3d Division commander and his staff officers boarded three armored vehicles in an effort to catch up with his own withdrawing column of troops. This occurred while U.S. helicopters came in to rescue the division's advisory personnel and their Vietnamese employees.

The 3d Division commander's attempt to join his column failed. Route QL-1 was clogged by refugees and battered troops, and all types of vehicles, military and civilian, frantically finding their way into Hue under the most barbarous barrages of enemy interdiction fire.

General Giai was forced to return to the old citadel and later he and his small staff were picked up by U.S. helicopters. When the last "jolly green giant" lifted off at 1655 hours with the 3d Division's senior adviser aboard, it was fired upon by enemy small-arms. At that time, the first NVA troops had already penetrated the Quang Tri Citadel. Quang Tri City belonged to the enemy: it was the first RVN provincial capital to fall into Communist hands during the war.

On Route QL-1, the tidal wave of refugees intermingled with troops continued to move south. The roadway became a spectacle of incredible destruction. Burning vehicles of all types, trucks, armored vehicles, civilian buses and cars jammed the highway and forced all traffic off the road while the frightened mass of humanity was subjected to enemy artillery concentrations. By late afternoon of the next day, the carnage was over. Thousands of innocent civilians thus found tragic death on this long stretch of QL-1 which later was dubbed "Terror Boulevard" by the local press. The shock and trauma of this tragedy, like the 1968 massacre in Hue, were to haunt the population of northern MR-1 for a long, long time.

Several ARVN units and the 147th Marine Brigade meanwhile managed to maintain some order in the midst of chaos and fought their way to the vicinity of Hai Lang. The 5th Ranger group, followed by the 1st and 4th moved on south to clear an enemy blocking unit. They were joined by the 1st Armor Brigade which took up night positions four kilometers southwest of Hai Lang. By late evening, remants of the 3d Division found their way to the vicinity of Camp Evans where General Giai had arrived. He was attempting to reestablish his headquarters and reorganize his units.

On 2 May, the 1st Armor Brigade attempted to move south on Route QL-1 but came under heavy and continuous artillery fire. These Armor forces finally closed on Camp Evans approximately 25 kilometers south during the early afternoon. The 147th Marine Brigade meanwhile was also subjected to the same attack from the direction of Hai Lang as it moved southward at dawn. With tactical air support and the assistance of some tanks, this brigade during the late afternoon passed through the 369th Marine Brigade defensive positions on Route QL-1 at the My Chanh River.

The entire province of Quang Tri was now in enemy hands. This provided North Vietnam with the opportunity to accelerate its push into the province of Thua Thien and toward Hue.

CHAPTER III

Stabilization and Counteroffensive

The Defense of Hue

During the month of April while the 3d ARVN Infantry Division and its attached units were battling the NVA 304th and 308th Divisions in Quang Tri Province, the 1st ARVN Infantry Division fought back several attempts by the NVA 324B Division to gain control of the western and southwestern approaches to Hue City in Thua Thien Province. Hue City was undoubtedly the prime target of enemy efforts in this area. But the seesaw battles that in fact had begun in early March then continued throughout the months of April and May without any solid gains from either side clearly indicated that this was only a secondary front designed to contain the 1st Infantry Division and support the main effort in Quang Tri.

The 1st Infantry Division and territorial forces of Thua Thien Province acquitted themselves admirably in the performance of their tasks. Although their exploits remained on the fringe of the limelight which was being focused on Quang Tri and An Loc at that time and seldom mentioned by the press, their valiance and combat effectiveness enabled I Corps to keep the enemy in check on this western flank and maintain overall tactical balance throughout the most critical weeks of the enemy's Easter offensive. When this offensive was about to enter its second week and as ARVN reinforcements were being poured into Quang Tri Province to hold Dong Ha and the Cua Viet line, the 1st Division was maintaining a firm line of defense in the foothills area west of Hue. This line extended from Camp Evans in the north, where the 1st Regiment Headquarters was located, continued through FSB Rakkasan, then southeast through FSBs Bastogne and Checkmate and linked up with FSB Birmingham,

the command post of the 54th Regiment. The 3d Regiment was kept in
reserve to add depth to the defense. FSB Veghel meanwhile had been
evacuated since the outbreak of the invasion.

The area around FSB Bastogne and FSB Checkmate, which straddled
Route 547 leading east toward Hue, was under intense enemy pressure. By
the second week of April, both bases were unable to be resupplied by
road. Enemy pressure was especially heavy on the high ground northwest
of Bastogne and east of Route 547 which had been interdicted. On 11
April, the 1st Regiment of the 1st ARVN Infantry Division attempted to
clear Route 547 but encountered strong and determined resistance from
the NVA 24th Regiment which held fast in spite of heavy ARVN artillery
fire and B-52 strikes. Attempts to resupply the beleaguered fire support bases by helicopters and air drops were only partially successful
while the increasing number of wounded caused by daily enemy attacks-by-fire presented a critical medical evacuation problem.

The situation around FSB Bastogne and FSB Checkmate became serious
during the last two weeks of April. Enemy attacks-by-fire and ground
attacks had increased considerably and all five defending battalions
were down to 50 percent of combat strength. However, as the weather
improved, extensive VNAF and U.S. tactical air support kept the
positions from being overrun. The enemy in the meantime had brought
heavy artillery to the vicinity of Route 547 and these guns presented
an increased threat to Hue City.

On 28 April, elements of the 29th and 803d Regiments, NVA 324B
Division, attacked FSB Bastogne. Three hours later, they overran this
firebase forcing a withdrawal to the east of FSB Birmingham. Consequently,
FSB Checkmate became vulnerable and was also ordered evacuated during
the night. The loss of these bases exposed Hue City to a direct
threat of enemy attack. Intelligence reports indicated that the
NVA 324B Division was being reinforced in preparation for the push
toward Hue. At the same time, there was a significant buildup of
enemy personnel and supplies in the A Shau Valley and the 66th Regiment,
NVA 304th Division, was reported moving to the FSB Anne area, probably
on its way to Thua Thien Province.

With the fall of Quang Tri City and the major part of the province on 1 May, the enemy's pressure naturally shifted toward Hue. On that day, he launched a heavy ground attack against FSB King and rocketed Camp Eagle, location of the 1st Division Headquarters. By early evening on 2 May, FSB Nancy, the last friendly base in Quang Tri Province was forced to evacuate under heavy pressure after receiving enemy artillery and ground attacks throughout the day. Marine elements had to fall back to south of the My Chanh River where they established a new defense line guarding the northern approach to Hue City. This was the last withdrawal during the Easter invasion by the forward edge of the I Corps battle area in MR-1.

The first days of May thus found South Vietnam's strategic posture in one of its bleakest periods during the entire war. North of Saigon, An Loc, the provincial capital of Binh Long Province, was under heavy siege. In the highlands of MR-2, the defense of Kontum City was becoming increasingly precarious. In northern MR-1, all of Quang Tri Province now lay in enemy hands; and Bastogne, the strongest bastion covering the western flank of Hue City had just caved in.

Since the beginning of the offensive, the enemy's pressure in Thua Thien Province had been relatively light. But the fall of Quang Tri Province was a serious psychological blow that deeply affected the morale of troops and the local population. Confidence in the I Corps ability to defend and hold Hue was shattered and on 2 May, the exodus of panicky refugees toward Da Nang began to usher in disorder and chaos. In Hue City, throngs of dispirited troops roamed about, haggard, unruly and craving for food. Driven by their basest instincts into mischief and even crime, their presence added to the atmosphere of terror and chaos that reigned throughout the city.

It was amidst this confusion and despondency that I was ordered by President Thieu on 3 May to take command of I Corps. I had served in I Corps under General Lam and the disaster that occurred there was no surprise to me. Neither General Lam nor his staff were competent to maneuver and support large forces in heavy combat. Now this fact was apparent to President Thieu and, because my Corps area was

ARVN Defensive Position on the My Chanh River

I Corps Forward Headquarters, Hue Citadel

in a stable condition and enjoyed the President's confidence, he selected me to replace General Lam. I had been following events in I Corps since the offensive began and expected to be called upon. I had already selected the staff I would take with me when the President told me of his decision. From my headquarters of IV Corps in Can Tho, I flew to Hue that very afternoon with a few staff officers of my own whose abilities and dedication had earned my respect. My arrival in Hue was not unlike the return of a son among the great family of troops and fellow-countrymen of this city whom I had the privilege of serving not very long ago as commanding general, 1st ARVN Infantry Division. I was gratified to discover that the trust they had always vested in me was still lingering. This reassurance was what I needed most in this bleakest hour of history.

On 4 May, I immediately set about to restructure command and control. A Forward Headquarters for I Corps was established at Hue. It was staffed by senior officers who had solid military backgrounds, both in the field and in staff work, a rare assemblage of talents from all three services and service branches. I had wanted to make sure that they knew how to use sensibly and coordinate effectively all corps combat components and supporting units in a conventional warfare evironment. I placed particular emphasis on developing an efficient Fire Support Coordination Center (FSCC) which was to streamline the coordinated, effective use of all U.S. and ARVN fire support. A Target Acquisition Element (TAE) was also organized to exploit the tremendous power of the U.S. Air Force and U.S. Naval gunfire.

The establishment of I Corps Forward brought about a restoration of confidence among combat units. They all felt reassured that from now on they would be directed, supported and cared for in a correct manner. The U.S. First Regional Assistance Command (FRAC) under Major General Frederic J. Kroesen and his successor, Major General Howard H. Cooksey was most cooperative. Both gentlemen honored me with their esteem and friendship which I highly valued. Together we worked on outstanding problems of common interest with a pervasive spirit of teamwork, openness and enthusiasm.

On 5 May, I initiated a comprehensive plan for the defense of Hue. The plan was simple in its basics; its merit lay in the clear-cut assignment of missions and responsibilities to each I Corps subordinate unit. By that time, the only remaining forces capable of effective combat north of the Hai Van Pass were the Marine Division with its three brigades and the 1st Infantry Division of which only two regiments were left (the 54th Regiment had been seriously mauled in the battles for Bastogne). The Marine Division, under its new commander, Colonel Bui The Lan, was responsible for the area north and northwest of Thua Thien Province; its mission was to block all enemy attempts to penetrate Hue.[1] The 1st Infantry Division, still under Major General Phu, was made responsible for the area south and southwest of Hue, defending the approaches from the A Shau Valley. *(Map 6)* In addition to their primary defensive missions, both divisions were given a free hand to conduct limited objective attacks in order to destroy enemy force concentrations in their sectors of defense. My concern at the time was to provide for a defense in depth, to economize force, to create a realistic chain of command, establish strong reserves for each major unit, and integrate the regular and territorial forces, which so far had operated with little coordination, into the corps defense plan. I believed that my concept for operations would respond to all of these immediate requirements.

Following the implementation of this plan, I also initiated a program called "Loi Phong" (Thunder Hurricane) which, in essence, was a sustained offensive by fire conducted on a large scale. The program scheduled the concentrated use of all available kinds of firepower, artillery, tactical air, Arc Light strikes, naval gunfire for each wave of attack and with enough intensity as to completely destroy every worthwhile target detected, especially those files of enemy personnel

---

[1] The division's former commander, Lieutenant General Le Nguyen Khang, was offered the command of II Corps by President Thieu but he declined. He was later appointed Assistant Chief of the JGS for Operations.

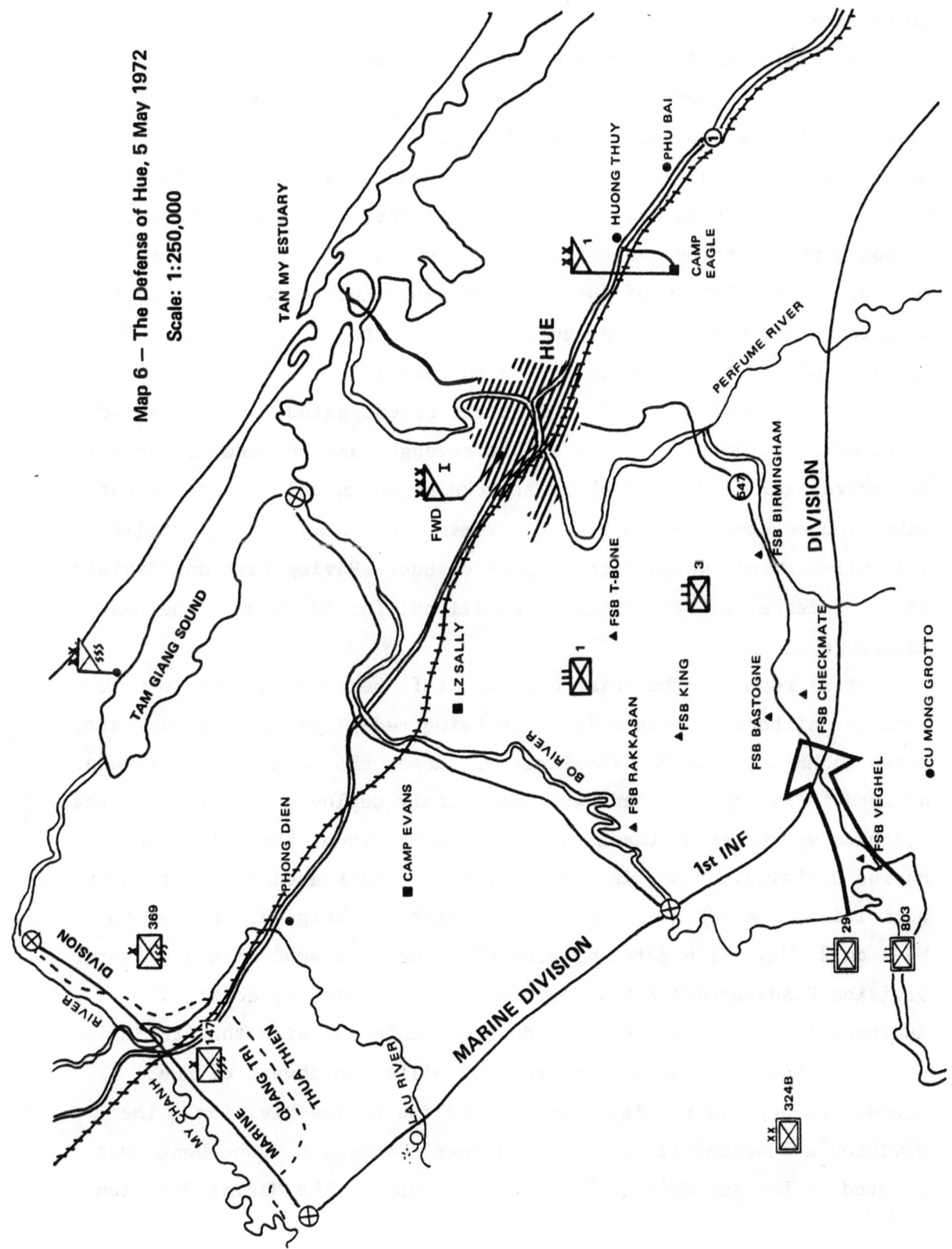

and materiels that were streaming toward staging areas near Hue. We hoped that his program would afford us the time required to complete the process of rebuilding and refitting those units which had disintegrated during the month of April.

By 7 May, our dispositions for defense in depth were well in place. Each unit, in the forward area as well as in the intermediate echelons, knew exactly what to do. The stabilization of the battlefield had an immediate effect on Hue City. Discipline and order were restored. Stagglers were picked up, placed under control and rehabilitated. Although the fighting was still raging and the situation far from secure, the population of Hue felt reassured enough to stay in place; even those who had evacuated began to return to the city. Life in the ancient capital began to return to normalcy.

In the meantime, spirited by their recent gains, NVA forces were endeavoring to build up their combat strength and prepare for an all-out drive against Hue. Probing attacks began in all sectors as our intelligence continued to report movements of enemy tanks, artillery, and anti-aircraft weapons converging on Hue. Having lost one division in the defense, I Corps required additional forces to meet the next challenge.

At my request, the Joint General Staff began to attach to my command the airborne forces which were being redeployed from other battle areas in MR-2 and MR-3. The first of these, the 2d Airborne Brigade, arrived in Hue on 8 May and was immediately deployed to reinforce the northern sector at My Chanh, under the operational control of the Marine Division. Soon, in keeping with the increased tempo of enemy activities, the JGS committed another airborne brigade, the 3d, to MR-1 on 22 May. I updated my plan of defense as soon as the Airborne Division Headquarters arrived and was placed under my control. I assigned it, minus its 1st Brigade but reinforced with the 4th Regiment of the 2d Division, an area of responsibility northwest of Hue, sandwiched between the 1st Division and the Marine Division. The division's headquarters, under Lieutenant General Du Quoc Dong, was located at Landing Zone (LZ) Sally. Meanwhile, the Marine Division assumed control of the 1st Ranger Group which had just been reorganized and refitted in Da Nang.

The rest of the month of May was a period of holding and refitting for I Corps forces. During this time, both the 1st Division and the Marine Division launched a series of limited but spectacular attacks from their forward positions. The Marine Division took the lead with a heliborne assault on 13 May during which two battalions of the 369th Brigade landed in the Hai Lang area, 10 km southeast of Quang Tri City, using helicopters of the 9th U.S. Marine Amphibious Brigade. After landing, the marines swept through their objectives and returned to their defenses at My Chanh. Caught by tactical surprise in his rear area for the first time, the enemy resisted weakly and incurred extremely heavy losses.

To compete with the marines, on 15 May, the 1st Infantry Division helilifted troops into Bastogne, caught the enemy offguard and retook the firebase while elements of its two regiments cleared the high ground south of the base and FSB Birmingham. A linkup was made the next day and ten days later, FSB Checkmate was back in friendly hands.

News of the reoccupation of these key strongpoints boosted the morale of ARVN troops and deeply moved an exultant populace. Never before had the solidarity between troops and the population in MR-1 been expressed with such effusion and spontaneity. The morale of I Corps troops rose to a high peak despite the lack of any organized program of motivation.

The fighting abated for about a week after the recapture of FSB Bastogne, then resumed on 21 May when the enemy struck in force against the marine sector in an attempt to regain the initiative. With a concentrated armor-infantry force, supported by several calibers of artillery, the enemy succeeded initially in breaking through the northeast line of defense. After intense fighting that lasted throughout the next day, the 3d and 6th Marine Battalions finally drove back the enemy and by nightfall restored their former positions along the My Chanh River. Even while these battles were being fought, the Marine Division completed plans for another major assault. In close coordination

An ARVN Antiaircraft Position Defending Hue City

Hue Citadel Bracing for Defense, 8 May 1972

with the 9th U.S. Marine Amphibious Brigade, naval gunfire and B-52 strikes, and the support of ARVN and marine artillery units, on 24 May the 147th Marine Brigade conducted an amphibious landing at My Thuy (Wunder Beach), 10 kilometers north of the defense line and simultaneously made a heliborne assault into Co Luy, 6 kilometers west of the coastline. Both elements swept through the enemy-held area and returned to the My Chanh line after several days of operation. This exploit was truly a historic event for the Marine Division which planned and executed an assault from the sea for the first time.

During the same period, the Airborne Division (-) which shared in the responsibility of defending the northwestern approached to Hue, made it possible for the Marine Division and the 1st Division to become more and more aggressive. By the end of May, the 1st Airborne Brigade arrived in Hue bringing the Airborne Division up to full combat strength. And so, within the space of less than one month, the defense posture of friendly forces in MR-1 had fully stabilized and became even stronger as May drew to its end.

It was quite a change from the bleakest days of early May when Hue lay agonized amidst chaos, terror, and uncertainty. Now there was cause to believe that Hue would hold firm in spite of the enemy's desperate but unsuccessful efforts to break through the marines' line. On 28 May, in front of the stately Midday Gate which opened on the Old Imperial Palace at Hue, President Nguyen Van Thieu affirmed this belief when he crowned the Marine Division's successes with a new star pinned on the shoulder of its commander, Colonel Bui The Lan. General Lan solemnly vowed to take back Quang Tri City from the enemy.

Refitting and Retraining

In conjunction with the efforts to defend Hue, an accelerated program of refitting and retraining was initiated for those ARVN units which had suffered severe losses or had disintegrated during the month-long enemy offensive. No effort was spared to reshape these shredded elements into combat-worthy units again. This was a high priority task dictated by I Corps force requirements to fulfill its mission and meet the challenge of regaining the lost territory.

ARVN casualties and material losses were severe. Several units had deteriorated to such an extent that they needed to be rebuilt from scratch. The 1st Armor Brigade alone had 1,171 casualties and lost 43 M-48's, 66 M-41's and 103 M-113's. A total of 140 artillery pieces were either lost or destroyed; this meant that about 10 ARVN artillery battalions had been stripped of all their equipment. The 3d Infantry Division had only a skeletal headquarters staff and the remnants of its 2d and 57th Regiments. All ranger groups suffered about the same casualties which amounted to over one half of their former strength.

Refitting efforts progressed rapidly and efficiently due to the dedication of ARVN logistic units under the Central Logistics Command and naturally, the quick and effective response of the U.S. logistic system under the supervision of MACV. Most equipment and material losses were quickly replaced. Among the most critical items were 105-mm howitzers, trucks and armored vehicles, individual and crew-served weapons, gas masks and other supplies such as artillery ammunition, fuses and claymore mines. All of these items were rushed to Da Nang by U.S. C-141 and C-5A aircraft or by surface ships. As a result, during this critical period no combat unit ever ran out of ammunition although the rates of expenditure had risen dramatically, especially in 105-mm and 155-mm HE.

To accelerate the retraining process, programs were shortened. A two-week quick recovery training program was conducted at each unit by ARVN and U.S. mobile training teams, usually at battalion level with all officers and NCOs attending. This program included both the theory and practice of marksmanship, handling of individual and crew-served weapons, reconnaissance and tactics. Particular emphasis was placed on the use of anti-tank weapons, especially the TOW missile, the first issue of which arrived on 21 May. Initially, the training for this missile was conducted by Americans from the 196th Infantry Brigade. Eventually, when this brigade returned to the U.S. training was continued at the Hoa Cam Training Center in Da Nang under ARVN instructors.

Artillery units, in addition to the two-week quick recovery program, also underwent special training courses on crater analysis and counter-battery fire, all conducted by U.S. Army targeting assistance teams dispatched from Fort Sill.

Several units, such as the 20th Tank Squadron, the 56th Regiment and the territorial forces (about 6,000 men) were required to undergo a complete refitting and retraining cycle. To facilitate control these units were assembled at two training centers, Dong Da at Phu Bai and Van Thanh on the outskirts of Hue. General Giai, who no longer had a command, was in Da Nang on 5 May when he was placed in arrest. Quite unfairly, but fully consistent with the practice in the ARVN, General Giai was held personally responsible for the defeat of his division. Although I would have been happy to have had General Giai resume command of the reconstituted 3d Division, I had no choice in the matter. I was barely able to save the name of the division, for I received many calls from the Chief of Staff, General Manh, who told me that President Thieu wanted the 3d removed from the rolls -- it was "bad luck" -- and to call the reconstituted division the 27th. The 3d Division, which was almost completely reconstituted immediately after the fall of Quang Tri, underwent a complete retraining program at Phu Bai. On 16 June, it relocated to Da Nang where security was more conducive to the rehabilitation process. While undergoing retraining there, it also assumed the defense of the city and an airbase complex relieving the U.S. 196th Infantry Brigade.

In general, the refitting and retraining process produced excellent results which, in a certain sense, were comparable to successes being achieved by our combat units defending Hue. The 3d Division in particular recovered rapidly under the strong leadership of its new commander, Brigadier General Nguyen Duy Hinh. Its return to the combat scene was truly a phenomenal achievement, according to unbiased comments by the RVN and U.S. military authorities.[2]

---

[2] Only a year later, in 1973, the 3d Infantry Division was rated by the Joint General Staff as the best among ARVN divisions. Its commander was also the only division commander to be promoted to the rank of Major General during the year.

President Thieu Visited the Defenses of the 1st Division

As the month of June drew to its end, I Corps forces had regained their former combat strength. They were now fully prepared to take on the challenge of driving the enemy from Quang Tri Province.

Quang Tri Retaken

One of the primordial tasks I Corps had to face immediately after the fall of Quang Tri was to regain the initiative. This was my primary concern when I took command. It was not an easy task, given the heavy losses, the deteriorating morale, and the precarious situation prevailing throughout the country at that time. The enemy was experiencing some problems too. His rapid success in Quang Tri, which he exploited skillfully, had advanced his forces too far ahead of his logistical capabilities. He needed time to resupply in the forward areas and meanwhile, airstrikes against his supply points and lines of communications were slowing this effort.

Stalling the NVA drive in MR-1 was just the first step. To hold back the onrushing tide, our lines of defense had to be consolidated and our forces redeployed and reorganized to exploit their offensive capabilities. Simultaneously and of equal importance, our troops had to be motivated by strong leadership not only to recoup their morale but also to become aggressive and imbued with an offensive spirit. This was what I began demanding from subordinate commanders, and as the situation improved, I encouraged them to plan limited offensive operations to keep the enemy off-balance. These operations, which were conducted during the months of May and June with a combination of heliborne assaults and amphibious landings, were well executed and achieved excellent results. Their effect on the enemy, coupled with devastating strikes by the U.S. Air Force and Navy, was astounding. Now off-balance and on the defensive, enemy forces were more concerned with their safety than the continuation of the offensive which was stalled. Our limited offensive operations had bought us enough time to prepare for the long-awaited big push northward.

The I Corps offensive campaign, code-named LAM SON 72, was

designed primarily to retake Quang Tri Province. It was conceived not as a blitzkrieg but as a coordinated and phased campaign combining the consolidation of the defense of Hue with successive offensive operations from our forward positions at the My Chanh line, first to destroy enemy forces, then to reoccupy Quang Tri City and finally to restore the provincial government. During the initial phase, our forces would attack to seize dominating terrain from which they could employ their fires to destroy all the enemy in zone. They would bypass political objectives, such as district towns unless it became necessary to enter them to destroy the enemy.

Preparations for the offensive were divided into three stages. During the first ten days of June, we repositioned forces across the front. From 11 to 18 June, the 1st Division launched an attack west in the direction of FSB Veghel while the Marine and Airborne Divisions conducted limited objective operations north of My Chanh to probe the combat strength of the enemy. From 19 to 27 June, a deception plan was initiated to confuse the enemy as to the timing and direction of the main effort. Under this plan, our forces made preparations for a fictitious airborne assault on Cam Lo and an amphibious landing on Cua Viet to cut off the enemy's supply lines and strike into his rear areas. Finally, two days before the big push, an intensive offensive by fire was to be conducted with B-52 strikes, tactical air and naval gunfire and artillery against enemy troop concentration areas, supply storages and gun positions.

LAM SON 72 was to be initiated on 28 June with a two-pronged attack northward coordinated with a supporting effort southwest of Hue. The Airborne Division would make the main effort, attacking on the southwest side of QL-1 toward La Vang, while the Marine Division would make the secondary effort along Route 555, moving toward Trieu Phong. The 1st Division, meanwhile, was to pin down enemy forces southwest of Hue. South of Hai Van Pass, in coordination with the northward push, the 3d Division was to continue ensuring the defense of Da Nang by conducting economy-of-force operations concerrent with its training and refitting program. In the meantime, the 2d ARVN Division was to conduct search and destroy operations in Quang Tin and Quang Ngai Provinces.

The plan was submitted simultaneously to Saigon by I Corps Headquarters and FRAC about two weeks before D-day. A day or so later, General Cooksey my senior adviser, told me that MACV had reviewed my plan and suggested that it would be better if I would continue limited spoiling attacks and consider a counteroffensive at a later date. This disturbed me greatly, for my troops were eager to go. I was ready, and it was a good, carefully worked-out plan. I decided to present it personally to the President, feeling confident that he would support it. He needed a victory in MR-1 to strengthen his political support.

I flew to Saigon and explained the plan in detail to the President, the Prime Minister, General Quang (the President's national security deputy) and General Vien. President Thieu listened, then, taking a purple grease pencil, drew an arrow on my map, suggesting a spoiling attack. The Prime Minister agreed, commenting on the French attack on the "street without joy." Discouraged, I folded my map and flew back to Hue.

I worried about this all night and very early the following morning called General Quang and told him that I would present no more plans to Saigon. If they wanted me to do anything, they should give me a Vietnamese translation of whatever plan they wanted me to execute and I would comply. The President called me about 0900 and told me that he was concerned about my plan -- that he felt it was too ambitious -- but that he would like me to return to Saigon and show it to him again. This I did the next day and, after a brief discussion, the President approved the plan.

LAM SON 72 began on 28 June as planned. Both the airborne and marine spearheads made good progress but slower than we expected. Enemy resistance was moderate during the first few days except for a few regimental-size clashes that occurred when our forces crossed the enemy's first line of defense north of the My Chanh River. However, as the enemy fell back and our forces advanced near the Thach Han River, his resistance became heavier.

On 7 July, the first airborne elements reached the outskirts of Quang Tri City where they clashed violently with the enemy defenders. The enemy was determined to hold fast and his forces were supported by heavy concentrations of artillery and mortar fire. To relieve the pressure on the paratroopers and also to interdict the enemy's line of communication with the city, along which he continually brought in more troops, I ordered the Marine Division to helilift a battalion two kilometers northeast of the city. This battalion was unable to make any progress, however; it was stopped by enemy infantry and armored elements.

By this time, the enemy's determination was all too clear; he planned to hold Quang Tri City to the last man. The enemy's ferocious resistance was such that Quang Tri City suddenly became a "cause celebre" that attracted emotionally-charged comments by public opinion throughout South Vietnam. Although it had not been a primary objective, it had become a symbol and a major challenge. The enemy continued reinforcing; he was determined to go all out for the defense of this city. The ARVN drive was completely stalled.

I Corps' position at this juncture was a difficult one. Pushed by public opinion on one side and faced with the enemy's determination on the other, it was hard-pressed to seek a satisfactory way out. My final assessment was that we could not withdraw again from Quang Tri without admitting total defeat; our only course was to recapture the city. Therefore, I directed a switchover of zones and assigned the primary effort to the Marine Division. The offensive then took on a new concept but the mission remained the same. I concluded that if the enemy indeed chose to defend Quang Tri City and concentrated his combat forces there, he would give me the opportunity to accomplish my mission employing the superior firepower of our American ally.

I modified the plan accordingly. *(Map 7)* The Marine Division had the mission to destroy enemy forces in the city. To economize its forces, the division was to establish a firm defense line along Phase Line Gold and from there to launch limited attacks against enemy forces up to the limit of the Cua Viet River (Phase Line Blue). The Airborne

Map 7 — Phase Lines North of Quang Tri

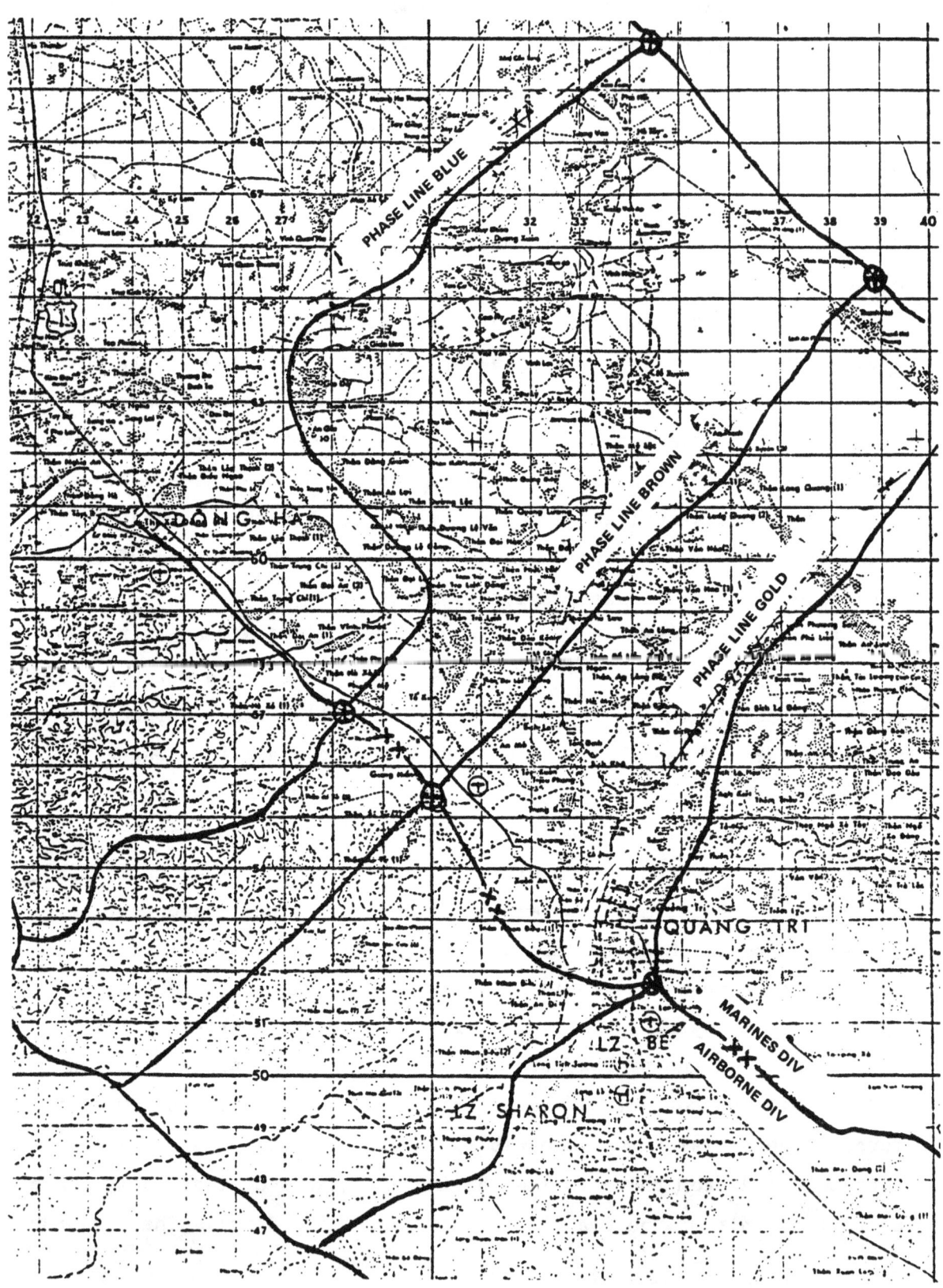

Division was to secure the Thach Han line and support the marines' effort. Its mission was to destroy the NVA 304th Division, reoccupy FSB Barbara and FSB Anne, interdict enemy supply lines from the west and protect Route QL-1, the I Corps main supply line.

Because of the enemy's determined defense, the recapture of Quang Tri City became a long, strenuous effort which carried into September. By that time, total enemy forces in Quang Tri and Thua Thien Provinces alone reached the incredible proportions of six infantry divisions, the 304th, 308th, 324B, 325th, 320B and 312th. The 312th Division had been redeployed from Laos and introduced into Quang Tri along with troop reinforcements for the other divisions. The showdown was inevitable. But the balance of forces was lopsided; the enemy had more than enough strength to contain South Vietnam's three divisions, even though they were our best ones.

In spite of continuous, violent clashes and the enemy's ferocious artillery fire which averaged thousands of rounds daily, I Corps forces were able to keep the offensive momentum going. This was possible because we rotated the frontline units, giving them a chance to rest and refit. The balance of forces, however, still favored the enemy heavily, which at times raised the question of whether we should reinforce MR-1 with additional troops. Consideration was even given to deploying an infantry division from MR-4, but the idea was finally rejected as neither feasible nor absolutely necessary. The military situation throughout South Vietnam during that critical period was such that the redeployment of a major unit would have seriously weakened the losing military region.

But neither the enemy's opposition nor the protraction of the campaign seemed to affect I Corp's tactical posture and determination. I believed that it was just a matter of time because all the ingredients for our success were there: a firmly established command and control system, a dedicated staff, and adequate support. The drawn-out contest between our forces and the enemy for this coveted objective might even be advantageous to us; if we had succeeded in retaking Quang Tri during the very first few days of the campaign, the battle area would not have attracted a sizable enemy force. Those six NVA divisions might have been diverted to the western approaches to Hue. This is what I feared most because our defenses in that rough terrain were more vulnerable. But concentrated as they were at Quang Tri, the enemy divisions presented lucrative targets for the combined fires of artillery, tactical air and B-52's.

When the offensive campaign entered its tenth week in early September without a decisive outcome in sight, I decided that the delay had been long enough. Enemy forces by that time had been reduced considerably by the volume of firepower delivered by B-52's, tactical air, artillery and naval gunfire; I was personally convinced that a new major effort by I Corps stood a good chance for success. A victory at this juncture would not only reinforce the RVN's military posture -- the enemy had been defeated at An Loc and Kontum -- it could also bring about excellent returns in a political sense.

On 8 September, therefore, I Corps launched three separate operations to support its major objective, retaking Quang Tri City. The Airborne Division advanced and reoccupied three key military installations formerly under ARVN control at La Vang, south of the Quang Tri Old Citadel. From these positions, the paratroopers were able to provide excellent protection for the southern flank of the marines. The next day, the Marine Division initiated the main effort, attacking the Old Citadel. At the same time, U.S. and RVN forces conducted an "incomplete" amphibious assault on a beach north of the Cua Viet River; the purpose was diversionary. At first, the enemy's determined resistance slowed the marines' progress, but elements of the 6th Marine Battalion penetrated one side of the citadel's walls on 14 September. During the following day, more marines were injected into the breach and other marine spearheads repeatedly assaulted the eastern and southern faces of the citadel. During the night of 15 September, the marines regained control of the citadel. Finally, in the morning of 16 September, the RVN flag was raised on the citadel amidst the cheers of our troops. This was a day of exalting joy for the entire people of South Vietnam.

By late afternoon of the next day, the marines had eliminated the last NVA remnants within the citadel and expanded control over the entire city which was now reduced to heaps of ruin. During the last ten days of fierce assaults on the citadel, 2,767 enemy troops were killed and 43 captured. Marine casualties during this time averaged 150 a day.

After Quang Tri City was retaken, the level of enemy activities throughout northern MR-1 dropped off markedly, especially in the marines' sector. This low activity level continued until 30 September when the Airborne Division again launched attacks to reoccupy FSB Barbara and FSB Anne. The paratroopers' attacks met with fierce enemy resistance. Their progress was slowed not only by heavy enemy artillery barrages but also by drenching monsoon rains. As October drew to its end, however, the Airborne Division finally reoccupied FSB Barbara and shifted its effort toward FSB Anne to the north.

In the meantime, the 1st Infantry Division sustained its initiative in Thua Thien Province. In addition to defending Hue, the division had the mission to conduct offensive operations to extend its area of control to the west and southwest. Activities in the 1st Division's sector were moderate during early June. They were mostly concentrated on the areas of FSB's Birmingham, Bastogne and Checkmate and along Route 547. By the end of June, however, enemy pressure bacame heavier.

During July, FSB Checkmate was subjected to heavy enemy attacks during which it was overrun and retaken several times. Toward the end of the month, FSB Bastogne also came under enemy control. For the first time in five months of hard fighting and under constant pressure, the 1st Division began to show some signs of weariness. Still, it held on to and maintained its line of defense. To help the division regain its vitality and aggressiveness, I decided to reinforce it with the 51st Regiment. Then, in early August, with the strong support of B-52 strikes and U.S. tactical air, the division successively retook Bastogne and Checkmate. During this month, as the enemy gradually lost his initiative, the 1st Division began to launch attacks to enlarge its control toward the west. Taking advantage of its renewed determination, the division even took back Veghel, the remotest fire support base to

The Author and MG H. H. Cooksey Beside the Symbol of Victory at Quang Tri City

NVA 130-mm and 122-mm Artillery Captured in Quang Tri

the southwest on 19 September. From then on, the NVA 342B Division completely lost its aggressiveness and avoided serious engagements. When October arrived, uninterrupted monsoon rains forced the 1st Division to revert to the defensive. Activities during this time plunged to the lowest level since the beginning of the enemy's Easter offensive.

From the time I Corps began offensive operations in Quang Tri Province to the end of July, the three provinces south of the Hai Van Pass were able to maintain reasonable control despite the low strength of friendly forces. Although sparsely used, B-52 strikes continued to be directed against a number of selected targets. However, as friendly forces in northern MR-1 approached Quang Tri City and were concentrating their efforts on this objective, the enemy suddenly chose to initiate several heavy attacks, especially in the area of the Que Son Valley, against elements of the 2d ARVN Infantry Division. This move was in all probability intended to alleviate our pressure on Quang Tri. Da Nang Air Base was also heavily rocketed many times. Enemy pressure was particularly strong on remote district towns in the foothills areas. Some of them were overrun after protracted sieges.

In the face of the enemy's mounting pressure, the 2d Infantry Division, now under Brigadier General Tran Van Nhut, was directed to concentrate its effort on the southernmost province, Quang Ngai, where the threat posed by the NVA 2d Division was increasing. Meanwhile, the 3d Infantry Division was assigned the mission to clear the pressure that the NVA 711th Division was exerting in the Que Son Valley and also to retake the district town of Tien Phuoc in Quang Tin Province. Despite superior enemy forces, both ARVN divisions were determined to fulfill their missions and performed extremely well. The successful operation conducted by the 3d Division to retake the district town of Tien Phuoc in particular -- its first major engagement since its battered withdrawal from Quang Tri not long ago -- truly marked its regained stature and restored to some extent the popular confidence vested in it.

Toward the end of October, the overall situation in MR-1 was completely stabilized. As the possibility for a negotiated cease-fire increased with every passing day, the people of Quang Tri, Thua Thien and Hue in particular rejoiced at the prospect of peace. But they all realized the great price that had already been paid for this possible cease-fire. Peace certainly would not have been obtained without the heroic exploits and sacrifices of the Marine Division, the Airborne Division and the 1st Division on all the battlefields of Quang Tri and Thua Thien. These exploits remained forever engraved in their minds.

Role of U.S. Air and Naval Support

During the entire period of the enemy's Nguyen Hue offensive campaign in MR-1, the support provided by the Vietnamese Air Force and Navy was marginal although they were employed to the maximum of their limited capabilities. Therefore, when the fighting broke out with great intensity and such a large scale, ARVN units had to rely mostly on support from U.S. Air Force and Naval units. This support was effective and met all of I Corps requirements.

Before April 1972, U.S. air activities in MR-1 were at a low level. Any 24-hour period with more than 10 tactical air sorties was considered a busy day. When the enemy's offensive began, however, U.S. air sorties increased dramatically. At one time, these sorties numbered 300 or more per day. Despite almost continuously bad weather during the month of April, air support was substantial and contributed initially to slowing down the advance of enemy forces and eventually stalling it altogether. B-52 strikes also increased remarkably during this period, averaging in excess of 30 missions a day. These strikes caused the most damage and greatest losses to enemy support activities. They were also used to provide close support to ARVN ground forces on several occasions. In addition to support provided the U.S. Air Force, I Corps forces also received much assistance from the U.S. Army 11th Combat Aviation Group whose activities were closely coordinated with those of ARVN units. This group provided essential support with troop lift logistical support and gunships.

During the early days of the enemy's invasion of Quang Tri, U.S. Air Force fire support missions were not only impeded by inclement weather but also by disorderly retreats of certain ARVN units. Since it was difficult for tactical aircraft to locate accurately friendly positions under those circumstances, large no-fire areas had to be established and this reduced the effectiveness of air support. As the weather gradually improved, and after the friendly line of defense had stabilized, air strikes became most effective against areas of enemy troop concentration, enemy tanks and artillery and lines of communication.

The NVA air defense effort increased during their invasion. At first SAM sites were located in the DMZ area along with antiaircraft guns but as NVA forces advanced south, they were also displaced south to the vicinity of Cam Lo and Route QL-9. Coverage by these missiles and guns thus extended to include our My Chanh line of defense. Throughout this forward battle area, enemy antiaircraft machineguns, artillery and SA-2 missiles were deployed in a dense pattern.

During May, coordination procedures for the use of air support were vastly improved after the relocation of I Corps Air Operations Center to Hue where it was co-located and operated in conjunction with the Fire Support Coordination Center. This provided much better coordination and timely control. In addition, tactical air control parties (TACP) were also deployed to operate alongside division tactical command posts. This newly arranged system of coordination and control, added to I Corps' gradual restoration of tactical initiative, greatly expanded the use of air support which totalled in excess of 6,000 sorties for the month. Enemy positions and artillery emplacements, particularly 130-mm guns, suffered severe losses; most spectacular were the results achieved through the use of laser-guided bombs and the technique of radar-guided bombing using aerial photo coordinates.

As to naval gunfire, its support was modest during the first day of the enemy invasion since only two destroyers, the USS Straus and USS Buchanan, were operating offshore MR-1 during late March. When the offensive broke out, however, all naval gunfire ships in the vicinity were immediately dispatched to the area and began providing support for the beleaguered 3d Division units. The level of naval gunfire support increased with every passing day. At one time during the month of June, there were as many as 38 destroyers and 3 cruisers on the naval gunline. The limited range of their guns however, still precluded the bombardment of targets located far to the west of Route QL-1. After the arrival of the heavy cruiser USS Newport News with her eight-inch guns during May, however, the destructive power and effective range of U.S. naval gunfire increased considerably.

Naval gunfire was particularly beneficial to the Marine Division. With its all-weather capabilities, naval gunfire responded perfectly to every support requirement within its range. During the period of I Corps stabilization and counteroffensive, the number of ships available for support varied from eight to 41 and the number of rounds fired ranged from a high of 7,000 to a low of 1,000 daily. For the control of fire, forward observer teams were attached to I Corps major units such as the infantry divisions, the 1st Ranger Group, and the Marine and Airborne Divisions and to the sectors of Quang Tin and Quang Ngai in southern MR-1.

In general, fire support available from U.S. and RVN sources was plentiful for I Corps throughout the enemy offensive. But the judicious and timely use of it proved to be a difficult problem in coordination and control. The establishment of a fire support center at Hue in May 1972 was a step in the right direction. For the first time, it enabled I Corps to integrate and make the most effective use of all U.S. and RVN fire support available. Because of its smooth operation, the center contributed significantly to the ultimate success of I Corps. It could be regarded as the symbol of effective cooperation and coordination, not only between U.S. and RVN elements, but also among our various services and service branches.

CHAPTER IV

Defending Kontum

The NVA Force Buildup

Adjoining the southern boundary of Military Region 1 lay the vast territory of Military Region 2, an area of sprawling high plateaus, rolling hills and dense jungle commonly called the Central Highlands, which sloped down toward a long, narrow, and curving strip of coastal land to the east. MR-2 was the largest of our four military regions, occupying almost half of South Vietnam's total land area. But it was also the least populated, with approximately three million people, about one fifth of them Montagnards. *(Map 8)*

Along the narrow coastland where most Vietnamese lived, ran National Route QL-1 which connected coastal cities such as Qui Nhon, Tuy Hoa, Nha Trang, Cam Ranh, Phan Rang and Phan Thiet. From the coast two major highways extended toward the highlands in the west: Route QL-19 and QL-21. Route QL-19 connected the port city of Qui Nhon with Pleiku and Kontum, two cities on the Kontum Plateau. Farther south, Route QL-21 connected Nha Trang with Ban Me Thuot, the only city on the Darlac Plateau. Both highways were important supply arteries for MR-2. Running the entire length of the highlands from north to south was Route QL-14 which originated from near Hoi An in MR-1 and connected Kontum with Pleiku and Ban Me Thuot. Because of frequent enemy interdictions, road communication between Pleiku and Ban Me Thuot was not always possible. South of the Darlac Plateau lay the Di Linh Plateau with its famous resort city of Dalat which was connected with Bien Hoa and Saigon in MR-3 by Route QL-20. Almost always a Montagnard area, this sparsely populated part of South Vietnam rarely attracted the interest of Vietnamese lowlanders.

Map 8 — Military Region 2

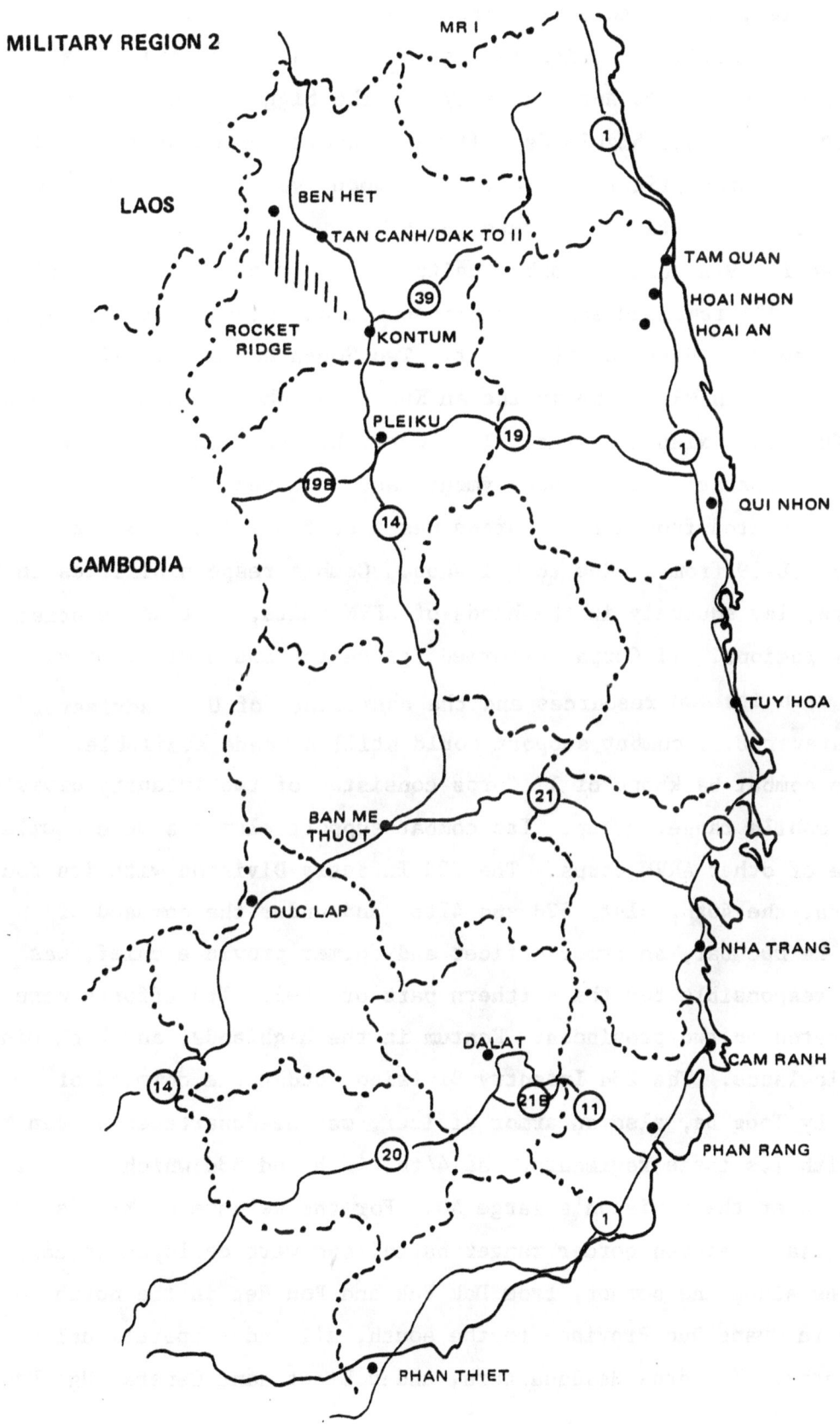

The weather of MR-2, under the reversible influence of opposing monsoon cycles, proved to be a fairly important factor that regulated the pattern of military activities on both sides. Over the years, the period from February to April usually saw the biggest increase in enemy activity in the highlands. It was a short period of fair and dry weather little affected by either monsoon cycle. The enemy did not deviate from this activity pattern in 1972.

By early 1972, all US combat units had departed the Central Highlands, but there still remained some logistic units and security forces at Qui Nhon and Cam Ranh Bases on the coast. Two South Korean divisions were still deployed in MR-2, one in the An Khe - Qui Nhon area and the other in the Tuy Hoa - Ninh Hoa area. They were, however, in a drawdown status in preparation for redeployment back to Korea. The most that could be expected from Korean forces was a continuation of security for Route QL-19 from An Khe to Qui Nhon. Combat responsibilities in MR-2 therefore, lay squarely in the hands of ARVN units, just as in other military regions. II Corps performed its search and destroy missions largely with its own resources and the assistance of U.S. advisers, plus whatever U.S. combat support could still be made available.

The combat backbone of II Corps consisted of two infantry divisions and one mobile ranger group. Its combat support elements were similar to those of other ARVN corps. The 22d Infantry Division with its four regiments, the 40th, 41st, 42d and 47th, and under the command of Colonel Le Duc Dat, an armor officer and former province chief, was usually responsible for the northern part of MR-2. Its efforts were concentrated on two provinces: Kontum in the highlands, and Binh Dinh in the lowlands. The 23d Infantry Division, under the command of Colonel Ly Tong Ba, also an armor officer, was headquartered at Ban Me Thuot with its three regiments, the 44th, 45th and 53d which were widely deployed over the division's large AO. For the defense of MR-2's long western flank, eleven border ranger battalions were deployed in camps and bases along the border, from Dak Pek and Ben Het in the north to Duc Lap in Quang Duc Province to the south, all under operational control of II Corps. II Corps Headquarters, under Lieutenant General Ngo Dzu, was located at Pleiku. In addition to its organic forces, II Corps occasionally received reinforcements from the RVNAF general reserve, usually airborne and ranger, when necessary to cope with increased enemy activities.

Starting in the fall of 1971, intelligence reports began to stream into II Corps Headquarters revealing the enemy's preparations for a major offensive campaign in the Central Highlands during the approaching dry season. Prisoner and returnee sources further disclosed that large enemy forces were moving into northern Kontum Province from base areas in Laos and Cambodia and their effort would concentrate on uprooting border camps and fire bases in northwestern Kontum, and eventually, "liberating" such urban centers as Pleiku and Kontum. In conjunction with this effort, the reports indicated, other enemy forces in the coastal lowlands were to increase activities aimed at destroying ARVN forces, particularly in northern Binh Dinh Province, where enemy domination had long been established. If these concerted efforts succeeded and joined forces, South Vietnam would run the risk of being sheared along Route QL-19 into two isolated halves.

In any event, the forces that the enemy would commit in this "Winter-Spring" campaign were substantial. Our intelligence sources had identified them as consisting of the NVA 320th and 2d Divisions and organic combat units of the B-3 Front, which would be the controlling headquarters for this highlands campaign. These units were supported by artillery and an entire NVA armor regiment, the 203d. This would, in fact, be the first instance of the enemy's employment of artillery and armor in the highlands. In the coastal lowlands, reports further indicated that disrupting activities would be conducted by the same old NT-3 "Gold Star" Division, augmented by Viet Cong main and local force units in the area. Finally, the enemy campaign was reported to be a multi-phase effort and the first phase could begin some time in late January or early February, the period of traditional Tet.

Faced with the impending offensive whose indications had already become too clear, our II Corps Command and the Second Regional Assistance Group (SRAG) under Mr. John P. Vann stepped up air and ARVN border ranger patrols. These reconnaissance activities were concentrated on enemy Base Area 609 which encompassed the Tri-Border corridor of infiltration and the Plei Trap Valley, some 55 km due west of Kontum City. In late January and early February, VNAF and U.S. air cavalry reconnaissance pilots repeatedly uncovered traces of large-scale enemy personnel and materiel movements in the area. Tracks of enemy tanks, perhaps a company of them were also discovered east of Base Area 609. At the same time, enemy documents seized by our patrols confirmed the presence of the NAV 320th Division in the B-3 Front's AO and revealed that the enemy had also introduced 122-mm and 130-mm artillery guns in the Tri-Border area. Consequently, B-52 and tactical air strikes were used to the maximum against targets detected, and ground operations by ARVN and territorial units were launched to search for the enemy. Simultaneously, II Corps began to reinforce the defenses of Kontum and Pleiku cities.

Intelligence reports on the enemy's buildup, especially on the presence of enemy tanks and artillery, greatly concerned Lieutenant General Ngo Dzu, II Corps commander. He reassessed all information available and after consulting with his adviser, Mr. John Paul Vann, whom he highly regarded and respected, General Ngo Dzu initiated a plan and began to redeploy his forces for the defense of the Central Highlands. He moved the 22d Infantry Division Headquarters, one of its regiments, the 47th, and a substantial logistic element of the division from their rear base in Binh Dinh Province to the Tan Canh - Dakto area. There, the division co-located its command post with the 42d Regiment, another divisional unit which had been deployed there for some time, near the junction of Routes QL-14 and 512. By 8 February, all movements had been completed. In addition, elements of the 19th Armored Cavalry Squadron were ordered by II Corps to Tan Canh to reinforce the division's organic 14th Armored Cavalry Squadron. Colonel Le Duc Dat, the division's commander, deployed some of these elements to Ben Het to block this likely approach of enemy armor. To reinforce the defense of Kontum, the 2d Airborne Brigade was also placed under control of II Corps to secure a string of fire support bases on Rocket Ridge which dominated Route 511 to the west and Route QL-14 and the Krong Poko River to the east, forming a screen protecting Tan Canh and Kontum City from western and northwestern approaches. The II Corps commander then delineated command and control responsibilities by assigning areas of operation to each of his principal subordinates, a technique similar to that employed in pacification. The 22d Division commander was given command responsibility over the Dakto area, to include ranger border camps at Ben Het, Dak Mot, Dak Pek, Dak Seang and Fire Support Bases 5 and 6. The province chief of Kontum was responsible for Kontum City while the II Corps Assistant for Operations, Colonel Le Trung Tuong, was to command defense forces in Pleiku. II Corps was thus fully braced for the enemy attack. *(Map 9)*

The expected attack did not materialize, however, probably because of II Corps' high state of alert and improved posture. The people of Kontum and Pleiku enjoyed an uneventful Tet which was disturbed only by a few scattered harassment incidents. In spite of the quietness, evidence of enemy preparations continued to surface and B-52 missions kept up preemptive strikes against targets of enemy logistic concentration northwest of Kontum.

The enemy meanwhile avoided direct engagements but increased activities against lines of communication and minor installations. It was as if he was marking time, waiting for the appropriate moment to strike. And again, he had acted quite contrary to our intelligence estimates which, based on the enemy's usual predilection for military action for a political objective, had expected that the offensive might take place before President Nixon's visit to China on 21 February, in order to discredit American prestige. Nevertheless, to ARVN military authorities, the comprehensive enemy preparations which were continuing unabated in Base Area 609 unmistakingly pointed toward a major action. This action had been withheld probably because the enemy was having some difficulty in moving supplies and troops into attack positions as a result of B-52 and tactical air strikes, or perhaps because weather conditions had not been favorable enough. In any event, a major confrontation with enemy forces in the northern Central Highlands was inevitable. It became now just a matter of time.

Map 9 — Western Highlands Battlefield

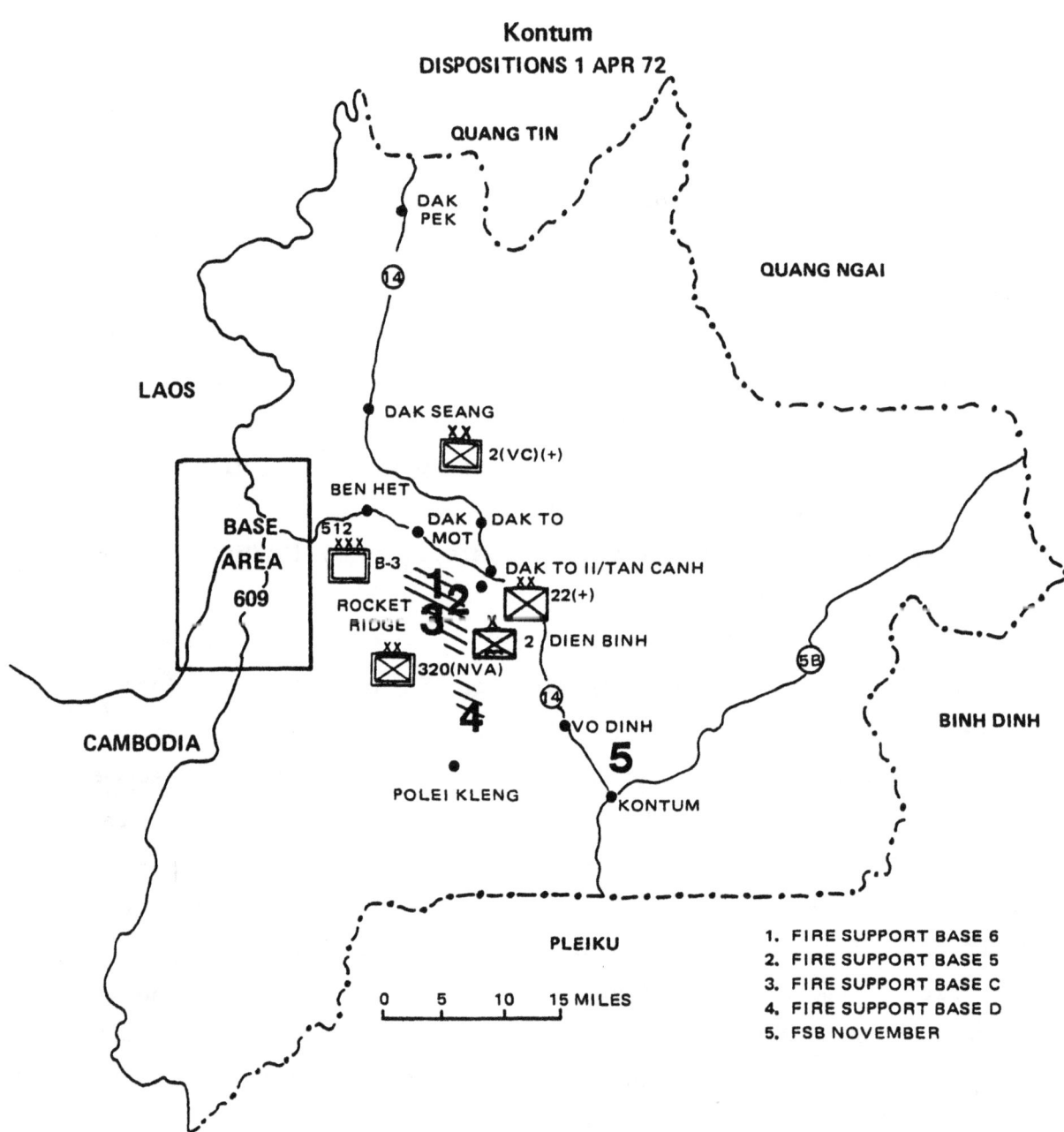

The ominous NVA buildup in MR-2 attracted the attention and concern of our Joint General Staff in Saigon. At II Corps request, therefore, another airborne brigade and the tactical command post of the Airborne Division—the last available reserves in the entire country—were directed to Kontum during the first week of March to assume the responsibility of defending this city and the southern area of the province. As reinforcements poured in, II Corps became more assured of its defense capabilities and initiated additional aggressive search and patrol activities in the suspected area northwest of Kontum as of mid-March.

During these operations, increased contacts with battalion and larger size units of the enemy 320th Division and 2d Division were made in the Rocket Ridge area and north of Kontum. Friendly forces, with the support of B-52's and tactical air, inflicted heavy losses on the enemy. During the first week of April, enemy assaults against fire support bases manned by ARVN paratroopers on Rocket Ridge again ended in dismal defeat and serious losses. These repeated enemy setbacks generated some doubts among II Corps staff as to the enemy's true capabilities to launch a major offensive as expected. They felt that the relentless use of B-52's and tactical air and the aggressiveness of friendly combat units had effectively delayed the enemy's timetable for offensive. This feeling was confirmed by depositions of enemy prisoners and ralliers who reported that NVA forces had indeed suffered extremely heavy losses in personnel and materiel as a result of B-52 strikes and contacts made with ARVN units. But they also revealed that the enemy continued to step up daily infiltrations to make up for the casualties incurred and to complete final preparations. Also, in early April, several enemy prisoners were captured during heavy clashes between the 22d ARVN Division forces and elements of the NVA 2d Division and B-3 Front north and east of Dakto. These sources disclosed that the enemy had reconnoitered ARVN defenses in the Dakto - Tan Canh area and was in the final preparatory stages for the offensive. The time for the attack was unknown but action was undoubtedly imminent.

These reports came at a time when in other military regions, NVA forces had already struck in force and obtained some initial objectives.

The II Corps commander, therefore, took this information most seriously and was deeply worried that perhaps his forces in the Dakto area were not sufficient to contain a major NVA thrust. Despite the apparent strain on logistic support for ARVN forces in that area which arose from a single road situation, General Dzu still made plans to deploy the 22d Division's remaining two regiments from Binh Dinh to Dakto. If this plan were put into effect, Binh Dinh Province, which was another important target being contemplated by the enemy, would be stripped of all ARVN regular forces. Mr. Vann thought that this would be most unwise. Anxious to obtain an overall tactical balance for MR-2 in case of concerted enemy attacks, Mr. Vann persuaded General Dzu to keep two regiments in Binh Dinh for the defense of the coastal area and to move the 23d Infantry Division's AO northward to southern Kontum Province in order to add depth to the defense of Kontum City. This seemed to lessen, but not dispel, General Dzu's excessive worries.

Thus the northern Central Highlands lay poised for the expected enemy attack which was surely to follow Quang Tri - Hue and An Loc. And if the enemy buildup in that area was of any indication, this attack would be at least as forceful as those already conducted on the other two fronts.

The Attacks on Tan Canh and Dakto

By the end of the second week of April, contacts with major NVA units had increased markedly and the area of Tan Canh - Dakto was virtually surrounded by enemy forces. On 14 April, Fire Support Base Charlie at the northern end of Rocket Ridge and 10 kilometers southwest of Dakto was heavily attacked by elements of the NVA 320th Division. In a classic conventional style, the enemy at first pummeled the base with heavy fire from assorted calibers, to include 130-mm and 105-mm artillery, 75-mm recoilless rifle, mortars and rockets. Then he launched two Korean-type massive assaults against the base, which was defended by an airborne battalion. In spite of vigorous and accurate support by U.S. tactical air and gunships, the enemy's overpowering pressure did not relent and forced the paratroopers to evacuate the base during the night after inflicting serious losses on the enemy forces. A week later, Fire Support Base Delta at the southern end of Rocket Ridge, also defended by paratroopers, was overrun by enemy armor and infantry after several days of heavy artillery fire.

Elements of the ARVN 42d and 47th Regiments in the meantime continued to operate in the Tan Canh - Dakto area in an effort to control surrounding ridgelines, but the enemy pressure gradually forced them to fall back to their bases at Dakto and Tan Canh. The 22d ARVN Division Commander's lack of determination to hold on to the ridgelines in the north and east which dominated the base area where his command post was located made the division's defense posture more vulnerable. His defenses had been practically reduced to the main base compound at Tan Canh.

Meanwhile, the Airborne Division tactical CP and an airborne brigade were ordered back to Saigon by the JGS on 20 April. They were replaced by the 6th Ranger Group redeployed from Hue and the 53d Regiment of the 23d ARVN Division which took over the AO vacated by the Airborne Division. At the same time, II Corps moved back some of its artillery elements in the Dakto - Tan Canh area to Dien Binh, six kilometers southeast on Route QL-14, apparently to provide more depth.

The 22d Division's defenses in Tan Canh, while appearing adequate, were in fact becoming precarious since the northern and eastern flanks had been left uncovered. The remaining fire support bases on Rocket Ridge appeared to be in the solid hands of the airborne brigade and the rangers but being located too far south, these bases were more useful to the defense of Kontum City than to Dakto - Tan Canh. In the immediate vicinity of Dakto - Tan Canh, there was only the 47th Regiment at Dakto II with a tank troop and an airborne battalion in support. The 42d Regiment was deployed on defensive positions near the compound occupied by the 22d Division tactical CP in Tan Canh and, although the 42d's reputation was one of the worst in the ARVN, its presence there added to the security of the CP. The 42d had been deployed at

Tan Canh for several weeks, and although Colonel Dat may have felt more secure with a better combat regiment protecting his headquarters, this was not an appropriate time to shift dispositions. Furthermore, it would have seemed illogical to place his least effective regiment farthest from the CP and in a position where it would be likely to be the first hit by the expected offensive. For two weeks, enemy artillery fire against the base complex in the Tan Canh - Dakto area had increased most significantly, averaging about 1,000 rounds daily. This fire was accurate, directed from high ground north and east of the Tan Canh compound and consisted of assorted calibers, from 82-mm mortars to 130-mm guns.

On 23 April, the attack began with a strong enemy force consisting of elements of the NVA 2d Division combined with B-3 Front units, sappers and tanks. The target was Tan Canh, which was defended by the 42d Regiment, two batteries of 155-mm and 105-mm, one M-41 and one M-113 troop and a combat engineer company.

During the attack, the enemy made extensive use of the wire-guided AT-3 "Sagger" missile which disabled our tanks and destroyed our bunkers with deadly accuracy. This was the first time our forces were exposed to this weapon and its use caught them and their U.S. advisers unprepared. One by one, the M-41 tanks positioned in defense of the division CP were hit and disabled along with several bunkers. Then the division tactical operations center took a direct blast at 1030 hours, burned, and had to be partially evacuated. All communications equipment was destroyed by the explosion. Without control and coordination, ARVN forces inside and outside the compound were left to fend for themselves. Morale and confidence had been dealt a devastating blow and rapidly deteriorated.

By noon, a makeshift division TOC was established by U.S. advisers at the 42d Regiment TOC with U.S. signal equipment. This helped the division command group regain some of its composure, but the division commander was visibly distressed. He declined to join the U.S. advisers at the new TOC and remained at his destroyed CP with his deputy, his aide, and some staff officers.

During the afternoon, ARVN artillery units opened counterbattery fire on suspected enemy gun emplacements without success. From the new TOC, advisers directed U.S. tactical air onto enemy targets based on reports from regimental advisers but bad weather and heavy enemy antiaircraft fire precluded accuracy and effect. The remainder of the day passed without significant events but when darkness closed in, enemy sappers destroyed an ammunition dump near the airstrip. Enemy artillery fire meanwhile increased markedly in intensity.

A few hours before midnight, Dakto district headquarters reported tanks approaching from the west. A Specter C-130 gunship was dispatched over the area; it located a column of 18 enemy tanks moving toward the district headquarters and engaged them with little success. At Tan Canh, reports of approaching tanks occasioned a flurry of defense preparations at the 42d Regiment; a major attack was apparently developing. At about midnight, reports indicated that tanks were moving south toward Tan Canh but no action was taken to stop their advance except for a short engagement by ARVN artillery fire which was rendered ineffective by heavy enemy counterbattery fire. The two bridges on Route QL-14 leading south toward Tan Canh were left intact.

When enemy tanks and sappers began attacking the 22d Division CP compound shortly before daybreak, it was already too late for any effective counteraction. After several days enduring heavy enemy artillery fire and taking many casualties, troops of the 42d Regiment were deeply shocked by the appearance of enemy tanks at the very gate of their compound. They fought in utter disorder, then broke ranks and fled through the defense perimeter.

Realizing that the situation had become hopeless, the division advisory team fought its way through enemy small arms fire and was extracted by an OH-58 helicopter with Mr. Vann aboard. By then the Tan Canh compound had become defenseless but Colonel Le Duc Dat, the division commander, and his deputy, Colonel Ton That Hung still remained within the old CP. They and their staff took time to destroy all radio sets and signal SOIs. In the afternoon, it began raining hard and they all took advantage of the rain to slip out. Since then, no one has ever learned with certainty what happened to Colonel Dat and his staff; they were presumably all dead. Only his deputy, Colonel Hung, managed to survive and reached Kontum several days later.[1]

At about the same time the enemy attacked the 22d ARVN Division Tactical CP at Tan Canh, several kilometers to the west, the 47th Regiment at Dakto II also came under heavy enemy pressure. The landing strip nearby was also attacked. On the division CP's orders, two armored cavalry troops and an infantry platoon left Ben Het in a hurry to reinforce the ARVN troops at Dakto II, using Route 512, the only roadway available, winding through hills and jungle. About half-way, after crossing the Dak Mot Bridge, the armor column was ambushed by a large NVA force holding the high ground just east of the bridge. Enemy anti-tank weapons destroyed all of the M-41 tanks which were the division's last reserves in the Tan Canh - Dakto area.

Without any hope for holding out successfully, the 47th Regimental headquarters and defending troops left the area in isolated groups. Subsequently, ARVN resistance faded away and the Tan Canh - Dakto area fell into enemy hands. During the next two days, NVA forces consolidated their gains and evacuated the thirty artillery pieces left behind by ARVN troops. They extended their control west of Dakto II and south to Dien Binh on Route QL-14.

In the meantime, the NVA 320th Division continued its pressure on the remaining fire support bases on Rocket Ridge. On 25 April, the II Corps commander decided to evacuate FSBs Nos. 5 and 6 because of their untenable positions. With this last protective screen finally removed, the entire area west of the Krong Poko River was abandoned to the enemy and Kontum City lay exposed to direct enemy attacks. NVA forces were now able to maneuver toward the city along Route QL-14 as the friendly

---

[1] Colonel Ton That Hung later retold his escape odyssey in a book he published under the title "Nguoi Ve Tu Tan Canh." (The Man Who Came in From Tan Canh).

positions in this area were evacuated one by one under heavy enemy artillery fire. As battered ARVN troops made their way south, they were joined by the local population while U.S. tactical air endeavored to destroy the positions and equipment they had left behind.

While the enemy was gaining ground in the Central Highlands and preparing to push toward Kontum, in the coastal lowlands of Binh Dinh Province, the NVA 3d Division and VC local forces cut off Route QL-1 at Bong Son Pass and attacked the three isolated northern districts, Hoai An, Hoai Nhon and Tam Quan. This forced the 40th and 41st Regiments of the 22d ARVN Division to abandon their two major bases, Landing Zones English and Bong Son, and other strong points in the area. Enemy attacks then spread out rapidly northward along Route QL-1 and southwestward along the Kim Son River, engulfing the district towns of Tam Quan and Hoai An in the process. In the face of the enemy's momentum, all defenses in the area crumbled rapidly.

With loss of Binh Dinh's three northern districts, the narrow coastal lowland of South Vietnam was practically cut in two, and if the enemy succeeded in taking Kontum City, then the defense posture of the country would look bleak indeed. Therefore, all attention now turned toward the Central Highlands where Kontum City was bracing itself for the inevitable NVA push.

In spite of the strong support of U.S. tactical air and B-52's, many ARVN commanders believed that Kontum could not hold. Lieutenant General Ngo Dzu was one of them. Distressed and demoralized by the loss of Tan Canh - Dakto, he felt remorseful about his refusal to reinforce Colonel Dat with the 22d Division's remaining two regiments. Had Colonel Dat not offered to resign his command the day before the attack just because he felt that he had not received adequate support?

General Dzu was doubtful that his remaining forces could contain the NVA multi-division push. He believed that Kontum City and even Pleiku, the seat of his own headquarters, would eventually turn into blazing infernos under the enemy's artillery and finally meet with the same fate as Tan Canh and Dakto. He thought of what had happened to Colonel Dat and he feared for himself. Tense, exhausted and unable to pull himself together, he spent his time calling President Thieu on the telephone day and night, begging for instructions even on the most trivial things. The big challenge had not come but the pressure had taken its toll.

To the JGS and President Thieu, General Dzu no longer functioned as a field commander capable of self-asserting command and control. He was finally replaced on 10 May by Major General Nguyen Van Toan, ARVN armor commander who was also serving as Assistant Commander for Operations, I Corps.

Pressure on Kontum City

During the days that followed the 22d NVA Division's debacle in Tan Canh, the enemy gradually moved his forces to the southeast toward Kontum City. The pressure he exerted on that city from the north was growing with every passing day. South of the city, the short stretch of Route QL-14 which connected it with Pleiku was also interdicted by solid enemy road blocks in the Chu Pao area and every effort to neutralize these blocks only added more casualties to ARVN forces. Kontum was thus isolated and surrounded. The final enemy push to take the city would surely occur as soon as he had built up enough supplies and combat forces in staging areas.

With battles raging in other places throughout the country, reenforcing Kontum City was becoming difficult. It was almost impossible now that all general reserves had been fully committed, here and elsewhere. Under such circumstances, obviously II Corps had to rely on the forces it presently controlled for the defense of Kontum. To meet the challenge, on 28 April, the 23d ARVN Division headquarters was moved approximately 160 kilometers from Ban Me Thuot to Kontum City to command of all ARVN forces in the area and reorganize them for defense. Security of southern MR-2 became solely the responsibility of the territorial forces.

II Corps' plan was to deploy four ranger battalions in blocking positions at Vo Dinh, 20 km northwest of Kontum, and along the Krong Poko

River southward to include Polei Kleng, a border ranger camp. To reinforce this camp, an important strongpoint that controlled the western approach to Kontum City, another ranger battalion was brought in.

The 53d Regiment, of the 23d ARVN Division, was responsible for the defense of the city itself. Time was pressing, and to gain enough time for the disposition of defense forces, the 2d and 6th Ranger Groups were given the mission to delay the enemy on Route QL-14 north of Kontum. In the meantime, B-52 strikes and tactical air were unleashed on enemy troop concentrations, particularly on the abandoned fire bases along Rocket Ridge.

The defense plan appeared to be sound and well conceived but there was still a problem of command and control. Colonel Ly Tong Ba, the 23d Division commander and defender of Kontum, was faced with difficulties in his exercise of operational control over various elements and units whose effectiveness had been adversely affected by the debacle at Tan Canh. Molding them into a cohesive defense force required more than his leadership could provide. For one thing, he commanded only one regiment, the 53d. Other units such as the ranger groups, the airborne brigade and territorial forces, although placed under his operational control, tended to maintain their own command channels with parent units. Colonel Ba's predicament was not unlike what General Giai of the 3d ARVN Division had faced in MR-1, though to a lesser extent. However, as far as the ARVN was concerned, here or elsewhere, operational control had proved difficult to exercise unless the field commander clearly outranked his subordinates or had an established reputation which commanded respect and submission. Colonel Ba apparently enjoyed neither.[2]

Meanwhile, the 2d Airborne Brigade which had been holding Vo Dinh since before the loss of Tan Canh - Dakto, was ordered back to Saigon.

---

[2] Although the TOE called for a major general to command a division, the practice of assigning colonels, brigadiers, and even lieutenant generals to these posts was widespread. This clearly caused serious problems, but the practice persisted. The rationale seemed to be that promising colonels should be given the opportunity to prove themselves, especially if they had powerful political sponsors.

This move left the 6th Ranger Group alone in the forward combat area with its battalions deployed on a high escarpment straddling Route QL-14 just south of Vo Dinh. On 27 April, the group CP was airlifted to FSB November, 12 kilometers southeast, just north of Kontum. On 1 May, the ranger battalions at Vo Dinh came under attack and were ordered to withdraw by the group commander. The ARVN defense line was thus moved back several kilometers to Ngo Trang, just 13 kilometers northwest of Kontum City.

This setback exposed the weakness of the command structure in Kontum. If this city was to hold, Colonel Ba's control would have to be strengthened. At the suggestion of Mr. John Paul Vann, General Toan agreed in early May to bring in the remaining units of the 23d ARVN Division, the 44th and 45th Regiments to replace the 2d and 6th Ranger Groups, respectively. This helped enhance not only Colonel Ba's command but also the overall effectiveness of the city's defense. Remnant forces of the 22d ARVN Division, meanwhile, were sent back to their rear bases in Binh Dinh Province for regrouping and refitting.

During this period, enemy attacks-by-fire increased substantially against those ranger border camps astride the NVA supply routes west and northwest of Kontum. Ben Het and Polei Kleng bore the brunt of these attacks because their positions obstructed the NVA movement of supplies into assembly areas for the attack on Kontum City. In spite of recent setbacks at Tan Canh, Dakto and Vo Dinh which to some extent had affected the morale of ARVN troops in the Kontum area, these isolated border camps held fast with support from the U.S. Air Force. But the enemy seemed determined to take Polei Kleng at all costs. On 6 May enemy artillery concentrated its fire on the camp, followed by ground assaults by the NVA 64th Regiment. Polei Kleng held on desperately for three days before the defending rangers were forced out by a massive tank-infantry assault on 9 May.

During these three days, B-52 strikes inflicted serious losses to NVA forces massed for the attack; the enemy paid a high price for the control of this western approach.

The rangers there resisted ferociously; they knocked out several enemy tanks and repulsed all ground assaults. Strangely enough, this lone and stranded outpost, the last one left dangling in a remote corner of Kontum Province, continued to remain under ARVN control until finally evacuated on 12 October.

Other ARVN positions of the 45th Regiment now assigned to delay the enemy on Route QL-14 north of Kontum also felt the mounting enemy pressure and gradually withdrew toward the city. At the same time, daily air reconnaissance missions reported new pioneer roads and new supply storage areas in the vicinity of Vo Dinh. Prisoners also confirmed on 10 May that the NVA 320th Division was moving into assembly areas north of the city.

Kontum now lay poised against the attack which could begin at any time. The enemy could not afford a long delay during which his concentrated forces would be vulnerable to U.S. air strikes.

The First Attack Against Kontum

By the end of the second week in May, the deployment of the 23d Division's units into positions in and around the city and their disposition for defense were completed. This disposition was essentially a perimeter defense with infantry and armor units blocking approaches from the north and northwest and territorial forces securing the southern and southeastern approaches, facing the Dak Bla River. The 44th Regiment was astride Route QL-41, about four kilometers northwest of Kontum, while the 45th Regiment defended the northern side of the city and the 53d, on the northeastern side, protected Kontum airfield. *(Map 10)*

In spite of this display of force, these defending units did not look impressive. Untried, their combat capabilities were very similar to those of the 22d Division. The 23d Division had yet to show that it was superior to its vanquished sister. But the division commander seemed to make a big difference. He personally inspected the defense perimeter with his staff, encouraged and provided guidance for his troops on tactical details and showed great care for them. The defense,

Map 10 – The Attack On Kontum

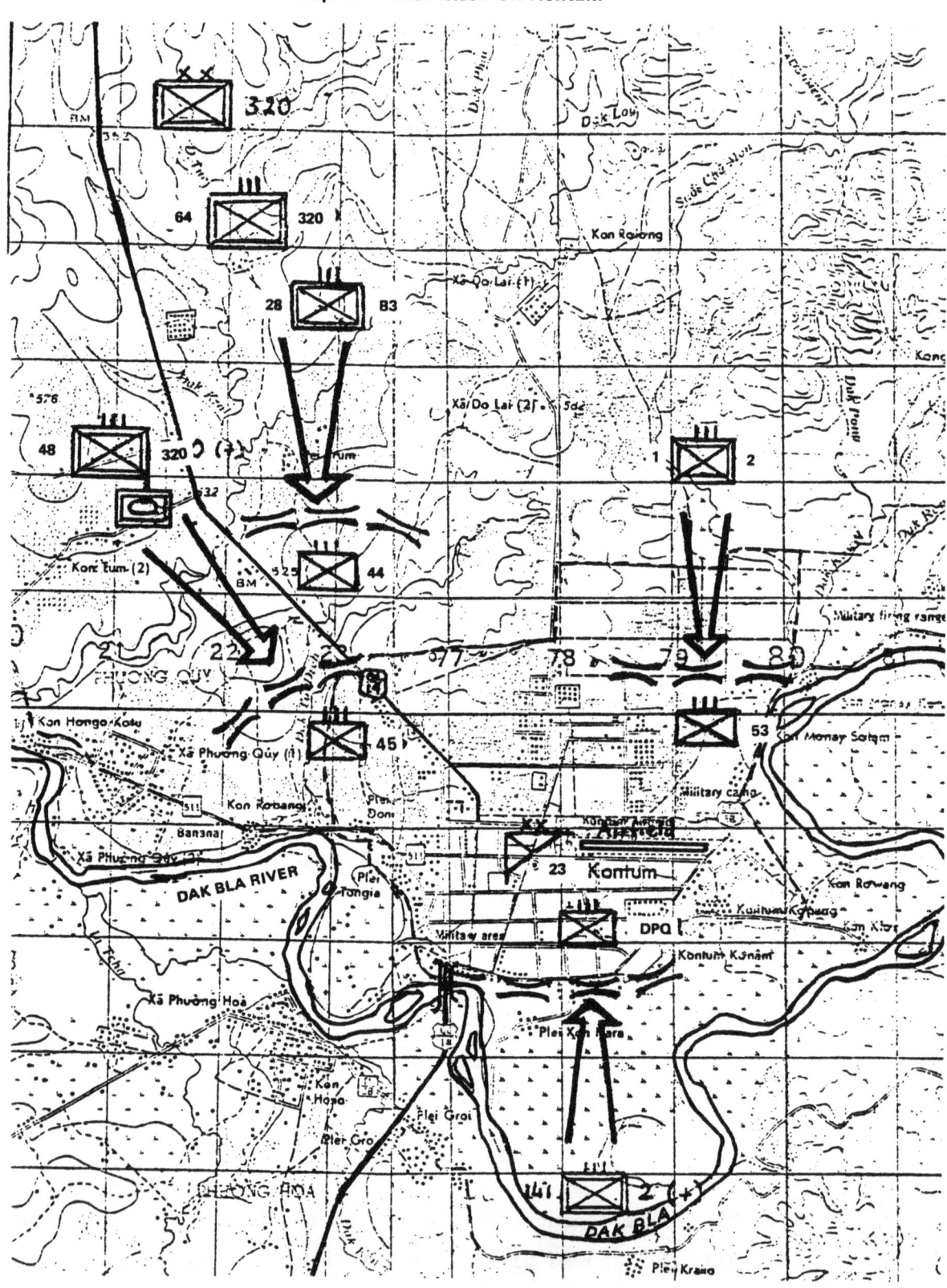

fire support and counterattack plans were coordinated and rehearsed daily, drawing on the painful lessons learned at Tan Canh. All units were given the opportunity to practice-fire the LAW antitank rocket until their troops became confident that enemy tanks were not as formidable as they had thought. More importantly, Colonel Ba's daily round of visits to his units greatly inspired his subordinates and instilled self-assurance among the troops.

In the early morning of 14 May, the enemy's attack on Kontum began. The defending forces had been alerted since midnight and they stood ready. ARVN and United States military intelligence in the meantime had been able to detect every enemy movement and even knew the precise time of the attack. Therefore, as the NVA troop and tank columns moved down Route QL-14 toward Kontum, U.S. Cobra gunships, some of them armed with the new TOW missile, were already airborne from Pleiku. Unlike the attack on Tan Canh, the enemy did not precede his advance with heavy artillery preparations except on FSB November. A total of five enemy regiments converged on the city. From the northwest the 48th and 64th Regiments of the NVA 320th Division approached with tanks forming two columns on both sides of Route QL-14. From the north, the 28th Regiment of the B-3 Front moved south against the ARVN 44th Regiment and the 1st Regiment of the 2d Division attacked the ARVN 53d Regiment, while the 141st Regiment of the NVA 2d Division attacked territorial force positions along the Dak Bla River south of the city. Despite its force, the initial attack was quickly broken up after several lead tanks fell easy prey to our artillery, LAW and TOW missiles.

Kontum City continued to receive sporadic artillery and rocket fire and ground probes during the day. The reactions of friendly forces had been quick, decisive and successful and the support of tactical air and gunships, most effective. ARVN armored elements, although at greatly reduced strength and held in reserve, had quickly maneuvered to fill in gaps in the defense perimeter. It seemed that the enemy would have a much more difficult time at Kontum than at Tan Canh just three weeks earlier.

As night approached, however, the enemy renewed his attacks with greater force against the 44th and 53d Regiments. Due to the confusion of night fighting which precluded effective coordination, an enemy battalion succeeded in breaking through a gap between the two regiments. This situation became critical when this enemy unit enlarged the gap and exploited its gains with successive waves of mass assaults. Even our concentrated artillery fire failed to stop the assaults and it looked as if the defense would soon meet with disaster. As the situation was becoming more precarious by the minute, Colonel Ba and his advisers worked feverishly on countermeasures.

The only way to turn back the large and growing penetration seemed to be B-52 strikes, two of which had been pre-planned for the night. Safety required however, that ARVN forces be pulled back one hour before the strikes. To fill this gap in time, increased and sustained artillery fire would be necessary. Both ARVN regiments were instructed to hold in place and move back on order. This was a bold and risky move but there seemed to be no other alternative to save Kontum from falling before dawn.

The two B-52 strikes came exactly on time, as planned, like thunderbolts unleashed over the masses of enemy troops. The explosions rocked the small city and seemed to cave in the rib cages of ARVN troops not far away. As the roar subsided, a dreadful silence fell over the scene. At dawn, ARVN search elements discovered several hundred enemy bodies with their weapons scattered all around. Kontum was saved.

Success in this first contest gave the defenders of Kontum added confidence. They believed that enemy forces were no match for the devastating firepower of the South Vietnamese and American planes and our artillery in spite of the enemy's numerical superiority and powerful tanks. They had seen for themselves how the NVA human wave assault was shattered by B-52 strikes. But it also dawned on ARVN commanders that their first success had really been a close shave and that Kontum might well have been in serious jeopardy had it not been for the two B-52 strikes.

In a postmortem examination of the results, Colonel Ba realized that there existed several weaknesses in his defenses. His units had been stretched too thin over the defense perimeter leaving gaps between them and making coordination difficult at limiting points. His staff had functioned well under stress but needed improvement, particularly in the coordination of firepower. So he set about tightening the defense by reducing the perimeter. He added some depth by moving the 44th Regiment back into a reserve position and replacing it with the 45th.

The new II Corps commander, General Toan and his adviser, Mr. John Paul Vann made a visit to Kontum City on 16 May. They reviewed the situation with Colonel Ba and approved his new disposition for defense. They also realized that despite his reverse, the enemy still possessed strong capabilities and he would surely launch another major attack in the next few days, perhaps with greater intensity.

In preparation for his next move, the enemy continued to probe the perimeter and hold Kontum under indirect fire. The division headquarters, artillery emplacements, and the airfield in particular attracted enemy mortar and artillery fire. Aircraft landings, even only for short refueling periods became hazardous and several planes were damaged or destroyed. Supply by air, therefore, was frequently interrupted and increasingly difficult.

Meanwhile, the enemy studied the defense system to find its weaknesses. He infiltrated sapper elements into the city by slippin- them through the southern defense sector which was manned by a hetero- geneous mixture of territorial forces, some of them from Tan Canh and Dakto. These sapper elements later posed a thorny problem for the defense. At the same time, other enemy reconnaissance elements and artillery forward observers managed to penetrate the city under the disguise of civilian refugees and ARVN troops. Using these fifth column tactics the enemy prepared to renew the attack combining the "noi cong" or inside force with the "ngoai nhap" or outside attackers. Kontum was a prize well worth these painstaking preparations.

By the end of the week following the first attack, all efforts by NVA forces to seize Kontum City had been defeated. Several times during this period, the enemy succeeded in breaking through our defense perimeter by violent assaults against positions held by the 44th and 53d Regiments and penetrating between the 53d and 45th Regiment. The dent made into the sector of the 53d Regiment on 20 May was particularly serious and had warranted the commitment of M-41 tanks held by the division in reserve.

Colonel Ba proved especially skillful in the maneuver of tanks, his own specialty for many years. His presence on the sites of battle also inspired his troops and helped them drive the enemy back. Elsewhere, the accuracy of ARVN artillery fire and the effectiveness of U.S. Cobra gunships, B-52's and VNAF Spooky gunships were instrumental in repulsing enemy assaults and penetrations. These successes enabled the restoration of the Kontum airfield to normal operation and the resupply of ammunition and fuel by U.S. C-130's.

His defense line stabilized and consolidated, Colonel Ba set about regaining some measure of initiative. With the support of U.S. tactical air and gunships, he launched several limited offensive operations in the areas north and northwest of the city within the range of ARVN artillery. During these actions, scattered contacts were made as troops discovered additional evidence of heavy enemy casualties caused by B-52 strikes.

From Pleiku, in the meantime, General Toan launched a major effort on 21 May to clear Route QL-14 north to Kontum. This vital supply road had been interdicted at Chu Pao Pass for several weeks by the NVA 95B Regiment. The II Corps relief task force consisted of the 2d and 6th Ranger Groups, augmented by armored cavalry and combat engineer elements. Despite the vigorous support of tactical air and artillery firepower, to include B-52 strikes and the use of CBU-55 bombs, the attack was slowed by multiple enemy blocking positions on both sides of the highway and finally stopped by a system of strong points entrenched on the rocky southern slope of the Chu Pao Mountain. Coordinated with the ferocious fire of concentrated artillery, this ring of enemy blocks inflicted serious losses and they continued to prevent road supply from Pleiku.

In addition to the attempt to open Route QL-14, II Corps also waged an intensive psywar and civic action campaign in the battle area, aimed at raising the morale of ARVN troops, enlisting the support of the local population and calling for enemy troops to defect. Refugees stranded in Kontum City were evacuated by increments to Pleiku for safety and better care. This helped improve control in the city; although under siege, Kontum did not face the chaotic ordeal that Hue had gone through previously.

In spite of the modest results achieved through its offensive efforts, II Corps had effectively upset the enemy's timetable for a last-ditch attempt to take Kontum. More importantly, II Corps had maintained the initiative and morale of its frontline troops both of which were most critically needed as the first signs of combat weariness began to show.

The Enemy's Final Attempt

After ten days of preparing his forces, the enemy resumed his attack on Kontum on 25 May. As the 23d Division commander had accurately predicted, this attack had all the intensity of a decisive, make or break effort. It had become imperative for the enemy to either achieve a quick victory or to withdraw his forces altogether for refitting. The drenching monsoon was setting in over the Central Highlands and its first effects had begun to be felt in the Kontum - Pleiku area. Even if he had the resources for replacements, a drawn-out campaign at this time could only spell disaster.

The attack began shortly after midnight with artillery fire pounding all the units of the 23d Division in the Kontum area. The firing concentrated particularly on positions near the airfield and south of the city. At 0300 hours, two enemy sapper battalions, with the assistance of elements already in place, began to infiltrate the southeastern positions held by territorial forces. They moved into an area near the airfield, occupied a school house, the Catholic Seminary and the Kontum diocesan office building. From the north and northeast, enemy infantry and tanks swarmed down and penetrated the city. Throughout the morning and into early afternoon, the division CP and artillery emplacements received continuous incoming artillery and mortar fire.

By late afternoon the enemy still held the areas within his penetration. The enemy's ferocious artillery fires during the day took a heavy toll. Among the artillery firing into the city were the 155-mm and 105-mm howitzers captured at Tan Canh. This fire was not only intense but it was also devastatingly accurate and it neutralized or destroyed a great number of our artillery pieces. The situation became so bleak that a tactical emergency was declared in order to divert all available tactical air and gunships to the area for the day.

During the next day, 26 May, enemy indirect fire increased and a coordinated attack by enemy tanks and infantry pressed against the 53d Regiment from the north. Pressure also mounted against territorial forces south of the city. With the support of Cobra gunships, a task force of one battalion of the 44th Regiment and eight tanks counterattacked and successfully contained an enemy penetration between the 45th and 53d Regiments. Still the enemy could not be ejected from the positions he had already seized. The situation remained stable for the day, however.

Meanwhile, supply shortages had become critical, since the airfield was closed to fixed wing aircraft, and the city's soccer field was used to accommodate CH-47 Chinooks hauling in emergency supplies and evacuating the seriously wounded. From the soccer field, VNAF helicopters shuttled supplies to the ARVN units north and northwest of the city.

At nightfall, the NVA 64th Regiment attacked again, penetrating between the 53d and 45 Regiments and concentrating its effort against the latter. Again, B-52 strikes, diverted from scheduled missions, fell on the forces attacking the 45th and helped blunt the attack.

In the early morning of the following day, 27 May, the enemy made a surprise thrust with two regiments and one tank company against the 44th Regiment held in reserve in the city's hospital complex. Fierce fighting ensued in and around this area resulting in a melee between enemy infantry and T-54 tanks on one side and ARVN troops and TOW missiles and ARVN LAW rockets. By late morning the enemy advance had been halted but NVA infantry still held the northermost compound and continued to harass the airfield.

From these and other positions across the northern part of the city, the enemy fanned out and formed pockets of resistance, particularly in areas where friendly use of fire was limited. Despite all the efforts of ARVN troops and the firepower of U.S. tactical air and gunships, and even the commitment of ARVN tanks held in reserve, it was difficult to dislodge the enemy from his positions. He seemed determined to dig in and exploit this foothold in the city.

To prevent further penetrations and consolidate his defense, Colonel Ba decided, with the approval of the II Corps commander, to tighten the perimeter again. He moved the 45th Regiment back from FSB November and positioned it on the reduced defense perimeter. This not only helped strengthen his defenses but also allowed for better use of B-52 strikes in close support.

By the night of the 28th, the situation remained critical. NVA forces were still entrenched in the hospital's northern compound and territorial forces were being engaged in house-to-house fighting in the southern area of the city where the enemy still held a school and a few houses near the airfield. By this time, however, the enemy began to run into difficulties in resupply. Hourly B-52 strikes had forced him to store supplies at great distances from the city and his transportation and communication lines were being disrupted by continuous airstrikes. The critical situation in the city also made friendly resupply and medical evacuation increasingly difficult but airdrops and CH-47 Chinooks from Pleiku nearby responded adequately to emergency requirements.

The attrition caused by airstrikes and gunships finally allowed ARVN forces to counterattack and regain the initiative. To dislodge the enemy, they had to fight from bunker-to-bunker, using hand grenades. Shortly before noon on 30 May, they regained control of the entire hospital complex and although there still remained other scattered pockets of resistance in the northeastern area, the city was clearly out of danger.

In the afternoon, President Thieu flew into Kontum City despite sporadic rocket and mortar fire. He praised the endurance and fighting spirit of all forces defending the city and right there, with the battlefield still rumbling, he pinned the brigadier general star on Colonel Ly Tong Ba, the defender of Kontum, for "special frontline merits."

Slowly but surely, during the remainder of the day, all positions held by the enemy were taken back. By midday on 31 May, the battle was practically over; the NVA main forces had withdrawn. Thousands of NVA bodies lay scattered all over the battlefield with dozens of T-54 tanks, some intact, but most reduced to charred hulks, awkwardly perched among the ruins. The enemy's final attempt to take Kontum had ended in utter defeat.

By 10 June, the last vestige of enemy resistance in the city had disappeared. But ironically enough, the man who had contributed so much to the ARVN success in Kontum -- Mr. John Paul Vann -- did not live long enough to savor the fruits of his labor on this day. A strikingly strong, though controversial personality, Mr. Vann was the personification of courage, selflessness and dedication. At Tan Canh, he personally directed, at extreme risks to his own life, the extraction of the 22d Division advisory team. His helicopter crashed at Dakto II but he continued his rescue mission undaunted. During the battles for Kontum, he saved the beleaguered city at least twice by making bold decisions on the use of B-52's. He goaded ARVN commanders on the battleline into action and shuttled almost daily, day and night, in and out of the battle area, with complete disregard for his own safety, to make sure that U.S. support for the defense was adequate. On one of his flights into Kontum City, the night before ARVN regained complete control, his helicopter crashed and he was killed. His replacement as chief of SRAG, now redesignated a command, was Brigadier General Michael D. Healy.

While the ARVN defenders were systematically eliminating all remaining pockets of resistance in the city, the NVA 320th Division withdrew toward Tan Canh - Dakto and continued the occupation of this area. Elements of the NVA 2d Division meanwhile returned to their former jungle redoubt in Quang Ngai Province, licking their wounds and recuperating. Subsequently, enemy activities in the Central Highlands dropped to a low level.

Riding on the crest of the Kontum victory, the General Toan successively launched clearing operations north and northwest of the city in an effort to reclaim the lost territory. In mid-June, the 23d ARVN Division conducted an airmobile raid into the Tan Canh area with its reconnaissance company. The objective was to create a psychological impact on the population living in the occupied area and to throw the enemy off-balance. Two more heliborne assaults were conducted during the following months but the objectives and results were limited.

Several ground operations were also conducted along Route QL-14 between Kontum and Vo Dinh to destroy enemy forces and enlarge friendly control during October. However, the limited capabilities of the division precluded any advance further than 10 kilometers northwest of Vo Dinh where ARVN control remained established until cease-fire day.

During the same period, other vigorous efforts were made to clear Route QL-14 between Pleiku and Kontum. Despite the enemy's fierce resistance in the initial stages, by the end of June the Chu Pao Pass area was cleared and the highway opened to commerical traffic in early July. The enemy continued to harass traffic with sporadic attacks by fire, however, and Route QL-14, although opened, remained insecure.

In the coastal lowlands of Binh Dinh Province, the 22d ARVN Division slowly regained its combat effectiveness after reorganization and refitting. In late July, in cooperation with territorial forces of the province, the division, now under Brigadier General Phan Dinh Niem, retook Hoai Nhon and Tam Quan district towns and reestablished communications on Route QL-1 north to the southern boundary of Quang Ngai Province. This accomplishment received little public notice but in terms of psychological, political and military impact, it equalled other ARVN successes such as the reoccupation of Quang Tri and the defense of Kontum.

CHAPTER V

The Siege of An Loc

The Enemy's Offensive Plan in MR-3

When the NVA crossed the DMZ and invaded Quang Tri Province on 30 March, the Joint General Staff was still having serious doubts about the enemy's real objective. Hue was apparently an immediate target. It had always been one of prime importance because of its historic stature. But evidence of enemy buildup in Kontum Province also presaged something serious in that area. The long-held theory that the enemy might attempt an attack across the Central Highlands to the sea to split South Vietnam into two parts was still in the minds of many Vietnamese and American strategists. If so, the Kontum Plateau could become another target of great strategic significance.

Little attention was being devoted to Military Region 3, however, although there was always the possibility of enemy offensive against Tay Ninh Province and perhaps Saigon itself. The enemy's disposition and capabilities along the entire western flank of South Vietnam, with his easy access to and from sanctuaries in neighboring Laos and Cambodia, made the problem of deducing the enemy's main effort all the more difficult. His advantage was such that the initial success of any thrust could quickly be reinforced and turned into the main effort; if not, it would serve some tactical purpose in support of other attacks. This flexibility was most likely what he had in mind when the southern arm of his Easter invasion struck Loc Ninh on 2 April.

Because of its proximity to Saigon by way of Route QL-13, the attack on Loc Ninh naturally raised the question of the enemy's ultimate objective. Was it Saigon, the capital, where all RVN military and political decisions were made?

Saigon was a large densely populated city with sprawling suburbs, and there were several avenues of approach, any of which could support a main attack. The northwestern and southwestern approaches were most important. From the northwest, an enemy attack could be initiated from the "Iron Triangle" area, which included such enemy bases as Ho Bo, Boi Loi and Long Nguyen. The avenues of approach would follow the Saigon River southward where it could be joined by another drive either along Route QL-1 from Tay Ninh or along Route QL-13 from Binh Long. From the southwest, the attack would originate in the Mo Vet (Parrot's Beak) and Ba Thu areas in Cambodia, then cross the Vuon Thom area in Hau Nghia Province and finally enter Cho Lon. This approach was the shortest.

Eleven provinces surrounded Saigon; among them Bien Hoa was by far the most important, being an industrial area and the site of III Corps Headquarters. Bien Hoa also contained a large Air Force base and the headquarters of the U.S. Army, Vietnam and the U.S. II Field Forces, both of which were located in the Long Binh base complex. The second most important province of MR-3 was Tay Ninh -- the holy land of the influential Cao Dai sect -- whose northwestern corner was a well-known enemy base area, Duong Minh Chau (War Zone C) which was the home and haven of enemy military and political leaders.

The field forces of III Corps consisted of three ARVN infantry divisions, the 5th, 18th and 25th and three ranger groups, the 3d, 5th and 6th. The 25th Division was assigned an area of operation encompassing the provinces of Tay Ninh, Hau Nghia and Long An, but the division headquarters and its three subordinate infantry regiments were usually located and operated in Tay Ninh Province. The 5th Division was responsible for the area of operation covering Phuoc Long, Binh Long and Binh Duong Provinces. Its headquarters was located at Lai Khe in Binh Duong Province. The 18th Division's area of operation extended over the provinces of Bien Hoa, Long Khanh, Phuoc Tuy and Binh Tuy. It was headquartered at Xuan Loc, the provincial capital of Long Khanh.

The military situation throughout MR-3 during late 1971 and prior to the 1972 Easter Offensive was especially good. The enemy's main force units, the 5th, 7th and 9th Divisions, had been driven across the northwestern boundary of MR-3 into Cambodia. Enemy border base areas such as 713, 354, 353 and 708 had been disrupted during the US-RVNAF cross-border operations in the spring of 1970 and they were no longer as active as in the past. To compensate, the enemy had established three new base areas deeper in Cambodian territory, Base Areas 711, 714 and 715. *(Map 11)*

During the period from January to March 1972, ARVN intelligence reported the presence of the NVA 5th Division in Base Area 712, near the Cambodian town of Snoul, about 30 kilometers northwest of Loc Ninh on Route QL-13. The other two enemy divisions, the 7th and 9th, were located in the Cambodian rubber plantation areas of Dambe and Chup, which were two of III Corps's operational objectives planned for the third quarter of 1971, plans which were suspended after the accidental death of Lieutenant General Do Cao Tri, III Corps commander. General Tri's successor, Lieutenant Nguyen Van Minh, advocated a strategy of standoff defense at the border instead of deep incursions into enemy base areas in Cambodia.

During this period, the ARVN commanders of III and IV Corps had independent authority to conduct operations deep into Cambodia, so long as they coordinated with their counterpart military region commanders in the Cambodian Army. They, of course, informed Saigon of their plans, but Saigon exercised practically no influence on the strategy each Corps commander decided to adopt.

All three enemy divisions were undergoing refitting and political indoctrination during the first quarter of calendar year 1972 but in late March we received the first information concerning a movement of the 9th NVA Division. It was provided by an enemy document captured during an operation in Tay Ninh Province.[1] According to the document,

---

[1] COSVN Directive No. 43.

Map 11 — Enemy Base Areas On Cambodian - RVN Border

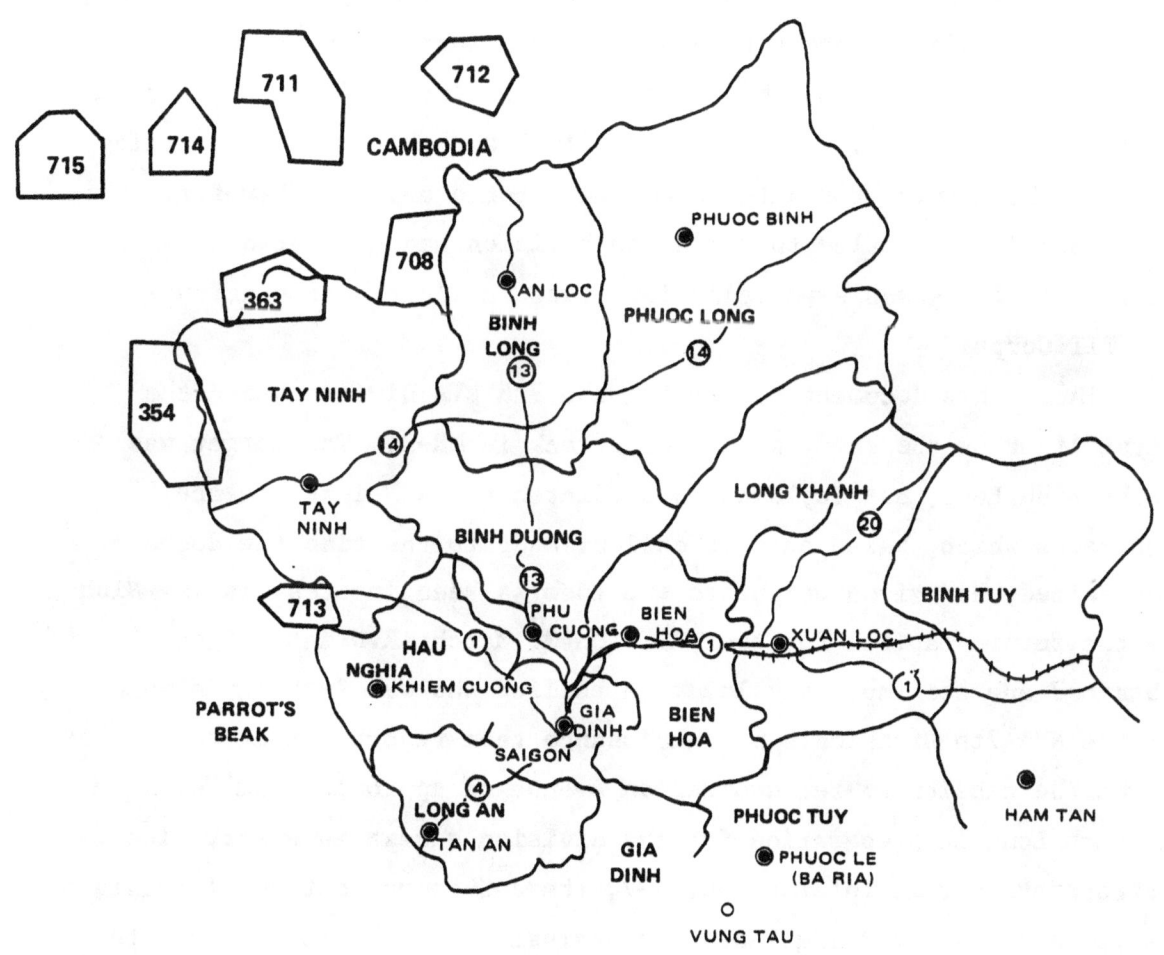

the 9th Division was planning to move to Base Area 708 in the Fishhook on or about 24 March and one element of the division was to assemble in an area southwest of the base. The 272d Regiment, 9th Division, would move into an area west of Binh Long to replace the division's 95C Regiment already redeployed, destination unknown. The document also mentioned an unidentified unit positioned north of the Tong Le Chon ranger camp. A very important fact revealed by this document was that the 7th and 9th Divisions were to coordinate actions for future campaigns and that troops and cadres of the 9th Division had received training in urban warfare. Finally, the 272d Regiment had received special training to conduct attacks against certain pre-selected targets.

The training of enemy troops for urban warfare was most significant because this training had been discontinued since 1969 in the aftermath of the Tet offensive. Not until late 1971 was this type of training known to be resumed for a few enemy main force units. Therefore, this document which revealed that the 9th Division had completed urban warfare training was especially important in planning the defense for III Corps.

Thus, this document concerning the 9th NVA Division shed the first light on the enemy's plan of attack in MR-3. The target was to be Binh Long, not Tay Ninh as predicted by ARVN intelligence estimates which, based on data collected up to the time the document was seized, had given weight to the enemy's keen interest in Tay Ninh as the future capital for the PRG. On 27 March ARVN intelligence obtained another important lead. A rallier who was formerly a member of the NVA 7th Division's reconnaissance team reported that he had been given the mission to reconnoiter an avenue of approach from Tay Ninh to Binh Long in preparation for the division's next movement. Then, corroborating this information, J-7, the JGS communications intelligence staff, also detected increased reconnaissance activities by the 7th and 9th Divisions in the boundary area between Tay Ninh and Binh Long Provinces. *(Map 12)*

In spite of these revealing pieces of information, III Corps Headquarters still did not focus adequate attention on Binh Long,

Map 12 – NVA Plan of Attacks in MR-3

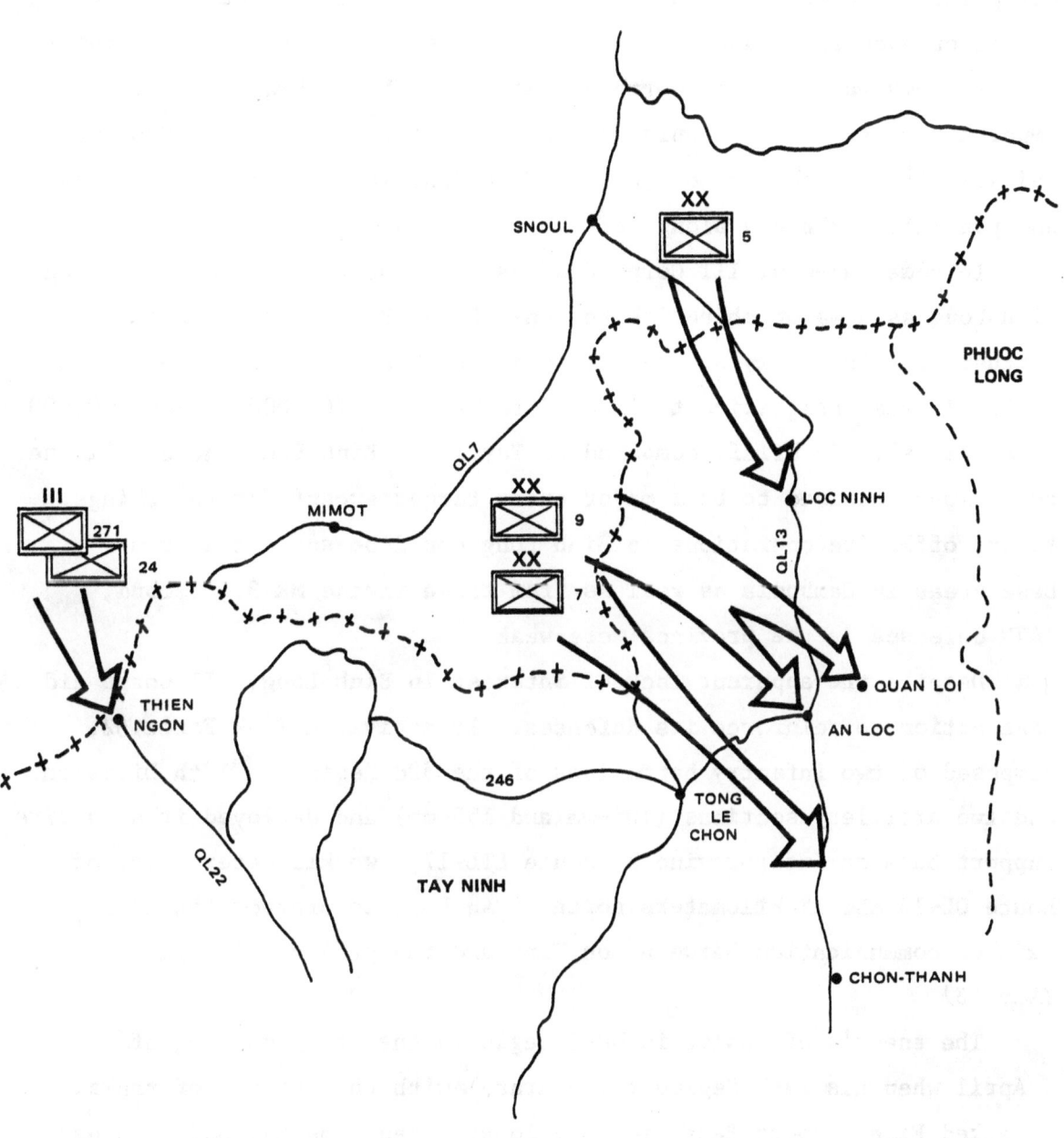

partly because the enemy had never shown great interest in this province. Although some major battles had been fought there in 1966 and 1967, these were more the result of the U.S. 1st Division's push up Route QL-13 -- and the 9th VC Division's response -- than COSVN's interest in establishing any political control in the province. Route QL-13 was certainly among the major avenues of approach into the Saigon area, but its importance to the enemy was slight north of Lai Khe. The highway was much more important to ARVN as the only ground link between Binh Duong Province, Lai Khe, Chon Thanh, An Loc and Loc Ninh, the major military defenses and population centers along it.

In some aspects, III Corps Headquarters was right in depreciating Binh Long as a major objective; for one thing, Binh Long was much farther from the enemy's border base areas than Tay Ninh. Demographically, it was insignificant compared to Tay Ninh (60,000 versus 300,000 inhabitants). In brief, compared to Tay Ninh, Binh Long lacked all the conditions required to be a major enemy target except for two things. First, offensive operations in Binh Long could be supported from base areas in Cambodia as well as from those inside MR-3. Second, ARVN defenses in the province were weak.

Despite the apparent lack of interest in Binh Long, III Corps did take action to reinforce its defenses. It activated Task Force 52, composed of two infantry battalions of the 52d Regiment, 18th Division and two artillery sections (105-mm and 155-mm) and deployed it at a fire support base on Interprovincial Route LTL-17, two kilometers west of Route QL-13 and 15 kilometers north of An Loc, to protect the main axis of communication between Loc Ninh and the provincial capital. *(Map 13)*

The enemy's offensive in MR-3 began in the early morning of 2 April when his 24th Regiment (Separate) with the support of tanks, attacked Fire Support Base Lac Long located near the Cambodian border 35 kilometers northwest of Tay Ninh City. This base was defended by one battalion of the 49th Regiment, 25th Division. The enemy's commitment of tanks contributed to the rapid collapse of this base which was overrun by midday.

Map 13 — Key Locations, Binh Long Province, MR-3

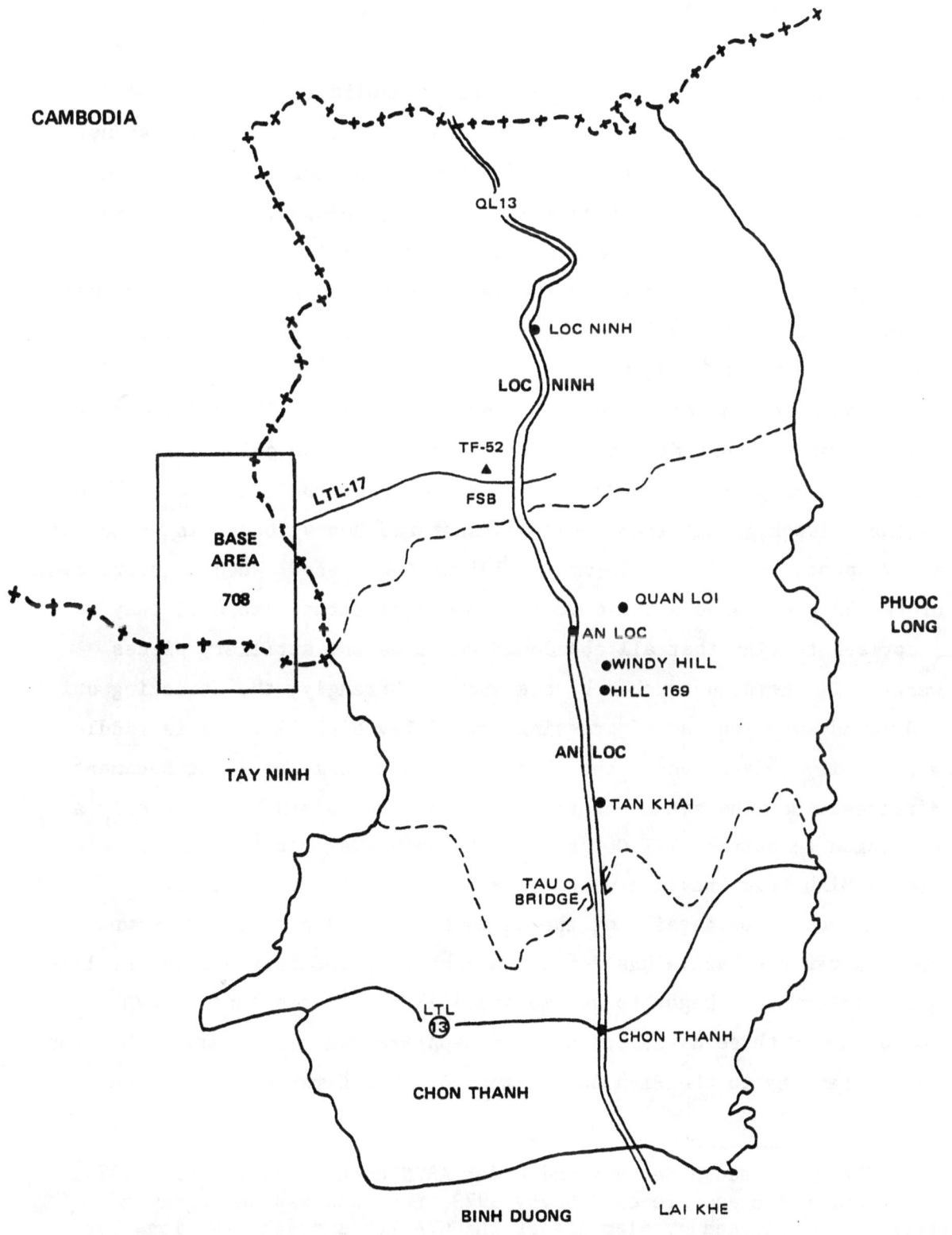

The rapid loss of FSB Lac Long prompted III Corps to make a quick decision to evacuate all advance outposts located along the Cambodian border. Since these small, remote outposts were difficult to hold against NVA main forces it was better to consolidate ARVN defenses deeper inside MR-3 in order to avoid losses in personnel and weapons. In rapid succession, all forces defending the border outposts, with the exception of one ranger battalion at Tong Le Chon, were ordered to fall back and establish a defense belt around Tay Ninh City. At the request of the battalion commander, who felt certain that his unit would become easy prey for an enemy ambush if it withdrew, III Corps consented to maintaining this border camp.[2]

Scattered contacts with the enemy were made by all border outpost elements as they withdrew toward Tay Ninh City. The defenders of FSB Thien Ngon, approximately 35 kilometers north of the city, were ambushed by the 271st Regiment (Separate) and suffered heavy losses in vehicles and weapons, especially 105-mm and 155-mm howitzers. When reinforcements of the 25th Division arrived at the ambush site the next day, they were surprised to find that all abandoned vehicles and artillery pieces were still there, untouched by the enemy. Strangly, the attacking unit had moved away instead of pressing toward Tay Ninh City. This riddle was finally solved much later when a prisoner from the 271st Regiment disclosed that the attack on the Thien Ngon defenders had been only a diversion to detract III Corps from the main NVA effort being directed toward Binh Long Province with Loc Ninh as the first objective.

Although the details of the enemy's plan did not become known until after the battle was joined in Binh Long and battlefield intelligence information began to accumulate, filling in the gaps, COSVN would commit three divisions and two separate regiments, all with armor reinforcements to the Binh Long campaign. The first phase was the

---

[2]Tong Le Chan Base remained under ARVN control until April 1974. Following the ceasefire of January 1973, the base was besieged and repeatedly attacked by elements of the NVA 7th and 9th Divisions for over one year before its final evacuation. It became a prominent case of enemy cease-fire violations and an eloquent testimony to ARVN combat heroism.

diversion in Tay Ninh, employing the 24th and 271st COSVN Regiments. The second phase would be the attack on Loc Ninh by the 5th NVA Division. The elite 9th NVA Division would then attack and seize An Loc, which would be turned into the capital for the PRG in South Vietnam. The NVA 7th Division, meanwhile, would block south of An Loc and prevent reinforcements from reaching An Loc. After seizing Loc Ninh, the 5th Division would march to Tay Ninh, isolate the city and destroy the forces of the ARVN 25th Division defending it.

The Attack on Loc Ninh

The attack on Loc Ninh began with an ambush on Route QL-13, five kilometers north of the town on 4 April. Ordered to fall back from the border to reinforce the defense of Loc Ninh, an ARVN armored cavalry squadron (-) attached to the 9th Regiment of the ARVN 5th Division was ambushed by an infantry regiment of the NVA 5th Division. Very few ARVN survivors managed to reach the district town. Early the next morning, the district defense forces reported hearing enemy armor on the move. A few hours later, the enemy began to shell heavily then attacked the Loc Ninh subsector headquarters and the rear base of the ARVN 9th Regiment located in the town.

The defenders resisted fiercely and employed the effective support of U.S. tactical air which was directed onto enemy targers by the U.S. district advisers. By late afternoon, the enemy's attempt to capture the Loc Ninh airstrip was defeated by CBU bombs of the air force. During the early hours of the next morning, 6 April, the enemy attacked again, this time with the addition of an armor battalion, estimated at between 25 and 30 tanks. Despite direct fire by ARVN artillery to stop the advancing tanks, Loc Ninh was overrun a few hours later. A number of survivors managed to break through and made it to An Loc; on 11 April, An Loc received the first group of 50 ARVN solders. The next day, they were joined by the Loc Ninh district chief who was soon to be followed by his senior adviser.

While Loc Ninh was under attack, the ARVN 5th Division ordered the

52d Task Force to deploy one of its two battalions to the beleaguered district town as reinforcement. The next morning when this battalion reached the junction of Routes LTL-17 and QL-13, it came under attack. At the same time, the second battalion, which was clearing an area west of the fire support base, discovered an enemy unit preparing to conduct an ambush. This battalion inflicted heavy losses on the enemy. Immediately after that, the 52d Task Force Headquarters at the base began to receive heavy fire.

By this time, Loc Ninh had been overrun. The 52d Task Force was ordered to fall back by road to An Loc to reinforce its defenses, but it was intercepted and attacked at the same road junction. After incurring heavy losses, the 52d Task Force withdrew into the jungle and by using alternate routes finally reached An Loc. Although disorganized and battered, the task force contributed additional personnel critically needed at that time for the defense.

The Siege and First Attacks

Only after the enemy's attack on Loc Ninh had been initiated was the III Corps commander, General Minh, fully convinced that An Loc City would be the primary objective of the enemy offensive. He also realized that if An Loc were overrun, Saigon would be threatened because only two major obstacles would remain on Route QL-13 north of Chon Thanh and Lai Khe. Therefore, An Loc was to be reinforced at once and held at all costs.

General Minh acted rapidly. The 5th Division Headquarters, with Brigadier General Le Van Hung in command, and two battalions of the 3d Ranger Group were helilifted into An Loc. This movement was completed without difficulties on 5 April, but by this time, III Corps no longer had a reserve.

During a meeting on 6 April at the Independence Palace in Saigon to review the military situation throughout the country, General Minh pleaded his case for more troops for the defense of An Loc. His request was overruled by considerations given to the seriousness of the NVA attacks in MR-1 and the enemy's ominous buildup in MR-2. Most of the JGS general reserve forces had already been committed to these regions. The only alternative left to provide reinforcements for III Corps was to assign to it the remaining airborne brigade and an infantry division which could be redeployed from MR-4. The question arose during the meeting as to which of these units would be most appropriate for III Corps.

At this meeting, attended by all corps commanders, Generals Quang and Vien, as well as the president and prime minister, the requirements of each corps for reinforcements were discussed. When it was suggested that the 21st Division be deployed to reinforce I Corps, General Quang argued that the situation at An Loc was potentially even more serious than the problem in Quang Tri. If the NVA succeeded in establishing a PRG capital at An Loc, the psychological and political damage would be intolerable for the GVN. The president agreed and the subject of which IV Corps division would reinforce III Corps was discussed. Consideration was first given to using the 9th Division, but as IV Corps commander at the time, I suggested the 21st Division, for two reasons.[3] First, the 21st Division was conducting successful search and destroy operations in the U Minh Forest and it was particularly effective in mobile operations. Second, the 21st Division had once been commanded by General Minh; placing it under his control again would not only facilitate employment and control by III Corps but also bring out the best performance from the division.

On 7 April, the 1st Airborne Brigade was ordered to move by road from Lai Khe to Chon Thanh. From there, it was to conduct operations northward to clear Route QL-13 up to An Loc and keep this vital supply line open. When reaching a point only six kilometers north of Chon Thanh, still 15 kilometers short of An Loc, the brigade's advance was

---

[3] A decision had been initially made to deploy this division to MR-1 in an effort to retake the lost territory north of the Cam Lo River. But Lieutenant General Dang Van Quang, President Thieu's Assistant for Security was afraid the GVN would lose face if the PRG succeeded in installing itself at An Loc. Hence the decision was overturned and the 21st Division assigned to MR-3 instead.

stopped by a regiment of the 7th NVA Division in solid blocking positions entrenched in the Tau O area. The enemy was determined to dominate this road and interdict every attempt to reinforce or supply An Loc.

After taking Loc Ninh, the NVA 5th Division began moving south toward An Loc. Beginning on 7 April, the local population living in the vicinity and workers in rubber plantations nearby reported the presence of NVA regular troops. Very rapidly, all food items in local markets around An Loc, especially canned or dried food began to disappear from display counters. Intelligence reports indicated that the enemy's rear services had preempted these food items to keep the combat units supplied while moving toward the next battlefield.

The city itself was not yet under attack but the Quan Loi airstrip, three kilometers east, came under fire and infantry assaults during the evening of 7 April. The fierceness of this attack was such that two ARVN companies which defended the airstrip were ordered to destroy their two 105-mm howitzers and fall back to the city. Two days later they arrived at the edge of An Loc.

The loss of the Quan Loi airfield edged An Loc into complete isolation because both air and ground communication with the city had now been cut off. The high ground in the Quan Loi area which dominated the city from the east also offered the enemy good artillery emplacements and observation from which he could pound targets in the city with deadly accuracy. Despite this, the 9th NVA Division did not attack the city until several days later. The reason for this delay, as later learned from enemy prisoners, was that logistic preparations had not been completed to support for the attack. According to COSVN's planning, it should take about one week to destroy all border outposts and during this time, supplies were to be moved forward for the attack on An Loc. The sudden evacuation of border outposts by the III Corps commander had thrown the enemy's plan into disarray and the 9th Division was forced to delay its attack after it had moved into position.

By 7 April, An Loc was entirely encircled and without a fixed-wing airstrip. Between 7 and 12 April all supply missions were flown by VNAF helicopters and C-123's. The use of helicopters ended on the 12th when a VNAF CH47 was shot down by antiaircraft fire. From then until

19 April all supplies were dropped by the C-123s. To achieve accuracy, they had to fly at very low altitudes over the drop zone. On the 40th such sortie, a C-123 was shot down.

In the meantime, reinforced by the 21st ARVN Division under the command of Major General Nguyen Vinh Nghi, III Corps was able to deploy the 8th Regiment, 5th ARVN Division with its two battalions to augment the defense of An Loc. Movement of this 8th Regiment was completed during 11 and 12 April, all by helicopter. The defending force in the city by this time numbered nearly 3,000 men, including RF and PF troops. "Chinook" CH-47 helicopters were used extensively to move in more supplies and evacuate the wounded and refugees.

Within the city, the situation became more tense by the hour. ARVN patrols outside the perimeter reported increased and heavy contacts with the enemy in the northeast and southeast. Refugees pouring into the city reported sightings of enemy tanks and artillery. All indications for a large attack on An Loc seemed to have finally fallen into place by nightfall of 12 April. *(Map 14)*

During the early hours of 13 April, the enemy began to shell the city heavily. Then shortly after daylight, units manning positions northwest of the city reported several enemy tanks and vehicles moving toward the city. An AC-130 Spectre gunship on station engaged the enemy and destroyed one tank and four vehicles. Simultaneously, several other tanks were reported on the northern side of the perimeter. By 0600 hours, the first major attack had begun against positions held by the 7th Regiment on the west. The main effort seemed to be developing from the north, however, spearheaded by armored vehicles. Overwhelmed by superior enemy forces, the ARVN defenders on this side quickly fell back.

A remarkable highlight during the first few hours of fighting was the effective use of the M-72 LAW rocket. In fact, the first tank killed by the ARVN defenders during the enemy attack on An Loc was scored by a RF soldier. Word of this feat spread rapidly among ARVN troops and their confidence was greatly enhanced. It was as if in just a matter of minutes, the long-established fear of enemy tanks had

Map 14 — The Defense of An Loc, 12 April 1972

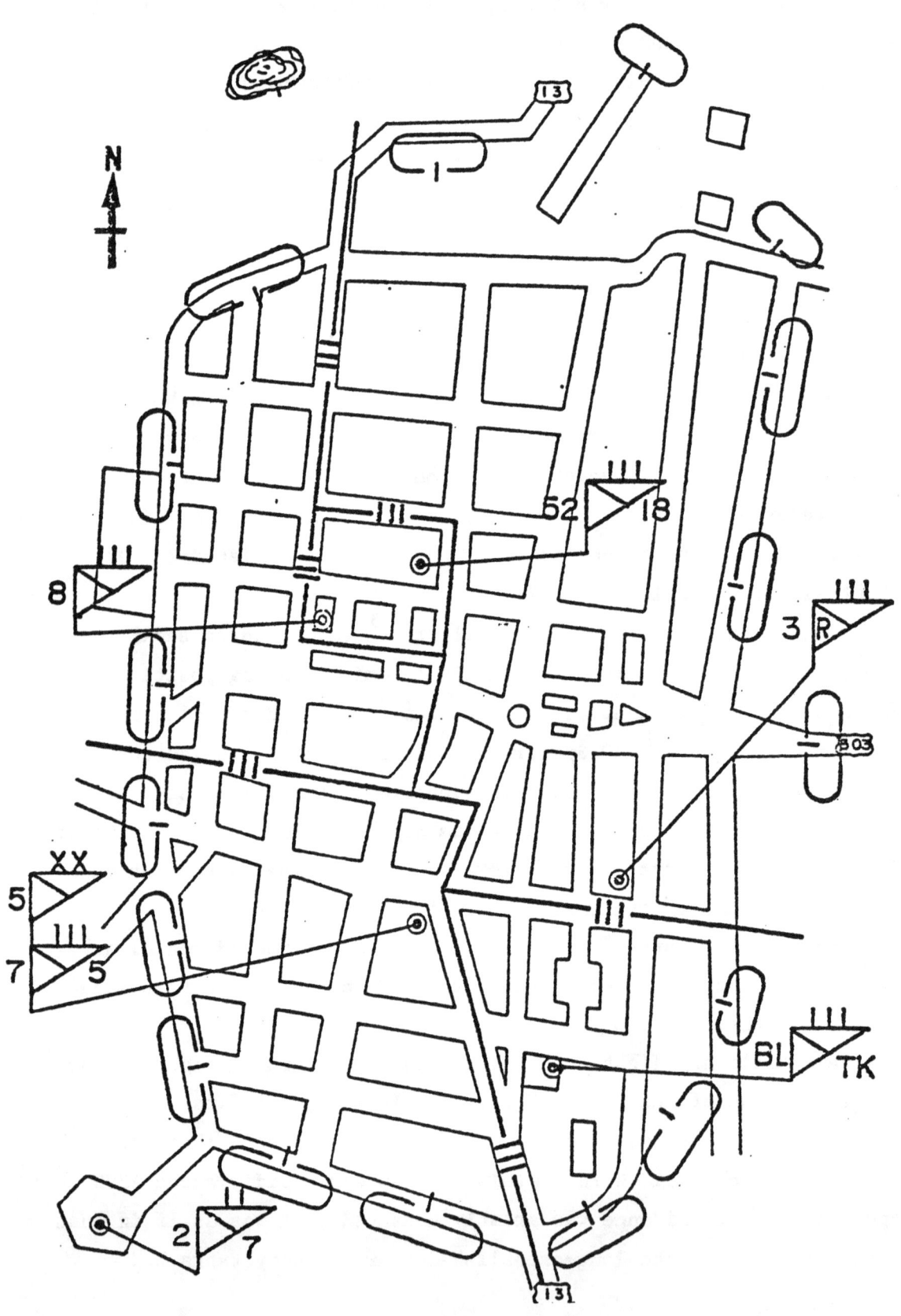

suddenly disappeared.

By this time, several enemy tanks had breached the defense and penetrated well into the city, but they remained isolated and no accompanying enemy infantry was in sight. One T-54 tank in particular rolled aimlessly through the city from north to south before it was destroyed by M-72 fire. Finally, four enemy tanks were knocked out and another one surrendered after its crew ran out of ammunition. Taken prisoner, one of the crew members declared he belonged to the 1st Battalion, 203d NVA Tank Regiment. His unit had moved from North Vietnam through lower Laos and then took shelter in Cambodia. His unit was ordered only the day before to move into Binh Long Province from the border and participate in the An Loc battle.

The III Corps commander appeared to be surprised by the presence of enemy tanks in Binh Long. He seemed to blame ARVN intelligence unduly for that surprise. However, in fact, as early as October 1971, ARVN intelligence reports had indicated the presence of enemy armor in the areas of Kratie, Dambe and Chup on Cambodia territory. In December 1971, the G-2 Division of the National Khmer Armed Forces General Staff also confirmed the existence of approximately 30 NVA tanks in Base Area 361, based on local informant sources. However, air photo missions had failed to record any traces of enemy armor movements probably since these movements were conducted at night. As a result, these ARVN and Khmer intelligence reports might not have convinced our III Corps commander.

The enemy probably considered the commitment of his tanks in MR-3 to be the key to success. He was certain that he could take Binh Long in five or ten days, and in any event no longer than ten days. To ensure success and because neither the 9th NVA Division nor its regimental or unit commanders had any experience with combined arms tactics, COSVN decided that COSVN Military Command would directly control the tank units. The results were disastrous. It was obvious that enemy tanks had led the attack and penetrated the perimeter without any support or protection from infantry units.

During 13 April, both the 271st and 272d Regiments of the 9th NVA

Division attacked in force. These attacks were met with strong ARVN resistance and the effective firepower of U.S. tactical air and B-52's. Enemy losses for this day alone amounted to nearly 400, over one half of which were inflicted by airstrikes. But the enemy was undaunted by these heavy casualties. He kept pressing his attacks during the next day, 14 April, preceding his armor advance in the early morning with heavy artillery fires. This time, his tanks were accompanied by small groups of infantry. One of these tanks came to within 500 meters of the 5th Division CP before it was disabled. Eventually, however, all enemy efforts during the day once again ended in failure.

After two days of fighting, the morale of the defenders remained remarkably high. They all seemed pervaded by the spirit of "holding or dying", determined to keep An Loc in friendly hands. This came from their conviction that they would never be left to fight alone and that they would be kept well supplied and reinforced as required. Their convictions were right throughout the battle for An Loc.

The 1st Airborne Brigade meanwhile had been withdrawn from the Tau O area, quickly refitted, and helilifted during 13 and 14 April into positions on Hill 169 and Windy Hill, three kilometers southeast of An Loc. The presence of paratroopers in the vicinity of the isolated city greatly encouraged the ARVN defenders and local population. Their confidence received an additional boost when they learned that the 21st Infantry Division from the Mekong Delta had reached Tau O on its way northward to relieve An Loc. So when the enemy resumed his attacks on 15 April with the support of 11 tanks, these tanks became targets for ARVN troops competing among themselves for quick kills. One of these tanks managed to reach a position where it fired point blank at the 5th Division tactical operations center, wounding the S-3 of Binh Long Sector and two other staff officers. When the dust of the battle cleared at day's end, 9 of the 11 tanks committed by the enemy had been destroyed.

The battle of An Loc abated somewhat on 16 April. After three days of combat, the enemy had lost 23 tanks, most of them T-54's and T-59's. However, the northern half of the city remained in his hands and his troops were facing ours, separated only by the main downtown boulevard. Also, the encirclement of the city seemed to be tightening.

The first enemy effort to take An Loc resulted in failure and COSVN modified its plan for the next effort. It decided to support the next major attack with a secondary attack against the ARVN 1st Airborne Brigade on Hill 169 and Windy Hill southeast of the city. This secondary effort would be conducted by two regiments, the 275th of the 5th Division and the 141st of the 7th Division. The main attack on An Loc would remain the 9th Division's responsibility. To minimize the effectiveness of our tactical air, the enemy also ringed the city with additional antiaircraft weapons.

The enemy's new plan of attack, however, came into our possession on 18 April. On that day, in an ambush laid on an enemy line of communication near Tong Le Chan Base, ARVN rangers killed an enemy and found on his body a handwritten report from the 9th NVA Division's political commissar addressed to COSVN Headquarters. This report analyzed the initial failure of the 9th NVA Division and attributed it to two major reasons. First, the intervention of U.S. tactical air and B-52's had been devastating and most effective. Second, coordination was ineffective between armor and infantry forces. The report also contained plans for the new major attack on An Loc which was to begin on 19 April. With this new plan, the enemy apparently believed An Loc could be seized within a matter of hours. So confident was he of success that on 18 April, a Hanoi Radio broadcast announced that An Loc had been liberated and that the PRG would be inaugurated in this city on 20 April.

In the early morning hours on 19 April, the enemy's attack proceeded exactly as planned and outlined in the captured document. While An Loc City came under heavy artillery and rocket fire, the NVA 275th and 141st Regiments attacked the ARVN 1st Airborne Brigade on Hill 169 and Windy Hill with the support of six tanks. This attack was so vigorous that the brigade headquarters on Hill 169 was overwhelmed and the 6th Airborne Battalion was forced to destroy its 105-mm battery and withdraw. Two companies of this battalion and the 1st Airborne Brigade Headquarters fell back to An Loc City. The remaining two companies were cut off and forced to move south; they were later picked up by VNAF helicopters and carried to Chon Thanh. All six enemy tanks were destroyed during the attack but the high ground dominating the city from the southeast was now in enemy hands.

Meanwhile the 9th NVA Divison's attack on the city itself again ended in failure. Its troops were unable to advance in the face of the determined ARVN defenders who still firmly held the southern half of the city. The enemy then modified his plan of attack, attempting to move southwest to Route QL-13 and attack An Loc from the south. This plan never materialized for the enemy discovered that on 21 April, his staging area, a rubber plantation just south of the city had been occupied by two battalions of the 1st Airborne Brigade who were firmly entrenched there. Unable to carry out the new plan, the enemy slackened his pace of attack which finally came to a halt on 23 April, ending in failure his second attempt to take An Loc.

Within the besieged city, friendly forces did not fare much better than the enemy, however. The northern half of the city remained in enemy hands. The enemy's defense in the northeastern quarter was particularly strong and unbreachable. The city's southern half meanwhile came under increasingly heavy attacks-by-fire everyday. On 25 April, the city's hospital was hit and destroyed. As a result, no medical treatment was available for our wounded, military and civilian alike. All casualties had to be treated in the areas where they were wounded. Medical evacuation in the meantime became impossible because of intense antiaircraft fire. The city was littered with bodies, most of them unattended for several days. To avoid a possible epidemic, our troops were forced to bury these bodies in common graves.

Supplies were running low; most critically needed were food, ammunition and medicine. Keeping the city resupplied was becoming increasingly difficult. Because of heavy enemy antiaircraft fire, our helicopters only occasionally succeeded in reaching the city and then only for emergency resupply missions.

Beginning on 20 April, all resupply missions were conducted by

USAF C-130's. The drop zone was the city's stadium, some 200-meters long, located south of the city in a relatively secure area.

The initial method used by the C-130's for airdrops was the HALO (High Altitude, Low Opening) technique. In this technique, the supply bundles were dropped from a safe altitude of 6,000 to 9,000 feet, and parachutes opened only at 500-800 feet above the drop zone. In the first eight HALO missions, most bundles fell outside the stadium and into enemy hands. This failure was traced to improper parachute packing by ARVN aerial resupply personnel who obviously lacked the technical training and experience required for the HALO method.

Since this problem could not be solved immediately, the USAF reverted temporarily to the low altitude container delivery method requiring daylight drops. But the C-130's were particularly vulnerable at low speeds over the drop zone and although they succeeded in delivering supplies to the ARVN defenders, the enemy's well placed antiaircraft fire caused considerable damage to almost every aircraft. These low altitude daylight missions were cancelled again on 26 April when one aircraft took a direct hit and exploded. Now it appeared that delivery at night was the only alternative pending a satisfactory solution to the HALO system. But night delivery had its own drawbacks in that the drop zone was difficult to identify in darkness even with marker lights. Various techniques were tried to improve delivery but did not provide desired results. The delivery rate therefore declined considerably and after a third crash, all resupply drops were discontinued on 4 May.

In the meantime, at the request of the Central Logistics Command, U.S. Army logisticians and USAF technicians had been working feverishly to solve the problem of parachute malfunctions. Two teams of qualified packers arrived from Okinawa to assist in packing and training ARVN personnel. Immediately, results improved. Two methods were tested on 4 May, HALO and High Velocity. Both proved remarkably accurate and as a result, aerial deliveries kept An Loc adequately resupplied until the day the siege was lifted.

During this time, our General Political Warfare Department had been especially active in enlisting popular support for the ARVN defenders in An Loc. No resupply missions to the besieged city were conducted which did not contain special gift packages from a grateful Saigon population. These gifts consisted of such delicacies as fresh vegetables and barbecued pork and stimulating personal letters of appreciation from schoolgirls. This solidarity action proved to have an excellent impact on the morale of the besieged defenders.

While resupply from the air proceeded without crippling problems, the recovery and distribution of supplies on the ground remained very difficult. Without coordination and control, it was usually those units nearest to the drop zone that got the most supplies. To solve this problem, the 5th Division commander placed Colonel Le Quang Luong, the tough 1st Airborne Brigade commander, in charge of recovery and distribution of airdrops.

Another difficulty which occurred during the recovery of airdrops was the problem of enemy artillery fire which was placed on the drop zone. As soon as a supply drop was made, the enemy immediately concentrated his fire on the stadium area. Consequently, very few soldiers or civilians volunteered to go to the drop zone to take delivery of the supplies. Only when enemy fire stopped was the recovery of supplies accomplished. This slowed down to some extent the entire recovery and distribution process.

Food and medicine received by ARVN units were usually shared with the local population. In return, the people of An Loc supplemented the ARVN combat ration diet with occasional fresh food such as fruit, vegetables and meat they gathered from their own gardens. In addition, they assisted ARVN troops in administering first aid and in medical evacuation and doing laundry for them. Never before throughout South Vietnam had cooperation and mutual support between ARVN troops and the local population been so successfully achieved as in An Loc. Among the ARVN units that earned the most admiration and affection from the city's population were the 81st Airborne Rangers and the 1st Airborne Brigade. Both of these units not only fought well and courageously but also proved particularly adept at winning over the people's hearts and minds.

There was little change in the situation between 23 April and 10 May. The ARVN defenders were reinforced by the 81st Airborne Ranger Group, an elite unit whose solid reputation in combat audacity and street fighting skills had been established since 1968. This unit was inserted by helilift into the southern edge of the city then moved on foot into the city and was given the mission to defend the northern part of what remained of An Loc. The deployment of airborne rangers into first line positions and of paratroopers at the southern edge made the defense of the city much stronger. The major ARVN concern now was no longer tactical but primarily logistical, particularly food supplies to feed the 4,000 ARVN troops and about 6,000 civilians in the city. If resupply became impossible then there would be the real danger of starvation.

The food supply problem became critical because the civilian population that remained in An Loc also had to share the infrequent airdrops. Most of the An Loc population had been prevented by the enemy from leaving the city. At first, however, the enemy encouraged the population to evacuate when he began to encircle the city. But realizing that the ARVN defenders would eventually run into difficulties with supplies and medical treatment if they had the responsibility for local inhabitants, the enemy reversed policy and prohibited the civilian exodus.

At the time the first enemy attack began, on their own initiative, some of the population of An Loc formed two groups and left the city. One group was led by a Catholic priest and the other by a Buddhist monk. Both groups moved south along Route QL-13 toward Chon Thanh. When they reached Tan Khai, a village located about 10 kilometers south of An Loc, both groups were stopped by the enemy. There, all able-bodied people, male or female, were impressed into enemy service as forced labor to move supplies. The remaining, children and old people, were all left behind to care for themselves. Abandoned and lost, they soon became prey to hunger and crossfire. They were finally saved from danger and death much later when ARVN troops came to their rescue.

The Second Phase of Attack

The enemy's preparations for the second attack on An Loc was detected as early as 1 May when the 5th NVA Division headquarters relocated south to Hill 169. The following day, two regiments of this division, the E-6 and 174th, also moved south. They took up positions on Windy Hill nearby where they joined their sister regiment, the 275th, which had been there since 19 April after the withdrawal of our 1st Airborne Brigade. Next, the 165th and 141st Regiments of the 7th NVA Division left their blocking positions in the Tau O area and moved to the southern and southwestern sectors of the city. These movements were detected and reported quite accurately by Airborne Radio Direction Finding (ARDF).

Together with the remaining units of the 9th NVA Division that continued to hold the northeastern portion of the city, this enemy redeployment was indicative of COSVN's determination to commit its entire combat force into an all-out effort to take An Loc. Facing these seven enemy regiments poised around the city, the ARVN defenders numbered fewer than 4,000. Although most were still combat effective, at least a thousand had been wounded. Morale was low since continuous enemy artillery bombardment kept the VNAF medevac helicopters away most of the time. Meanwhile, enemy deployments and an increase in enemy artillery and rocket fire against the city pointed toward an imminent all-out attack.

The new plan of attack was confirmed and other details were learned on 5 May when an enemy soldier surrendered to regional forces patrolling on the southern defense perimeter. He was a lieutenant from the 9th NVA Division. Interrogated, this enemy rallier reported that his division commander had been severely reprimanded by COSVN for failure to capture An Loc. In the meantime, COSVN's Military Command had approved the 5th NVA Division commander's request that his unit conduct the primary attack instead of the 9th Division. He promised he would take An Loc within two days, as he had Loc Ninh. The rallier also disclosed that the 5th NVA Division's effort from the southeast was to be coordinated with that of the 7th Division from the southwest and a supporting effort by the 9th from the northeast. He did not know the exact time of the attack but estimated that it would materialize within one week.

In the face of enemy intentions and known troop dispositions, the J2 and J3 at MACV began planning the use of B-52's to break the enemy's decisive effort. General Abrams, COMUSMACV, quickly approved his staff's recommendations and provided III Corps with maximum tactical air support and priority in B-52 strikes for the defense of An Loc. The problem with using B-52's in tactical support, however, was precise timing, and to break the enemy effort the first requirement was to know exactly on what day this attack would begin.

On 9 May, the enemy initiated strong ground probes and increased his artillery fire. The ground pressure abated within two hours but the heavy bombardment continued. To anyone knowledgeable about the pattern of enemy attacks in South Vietnam, this was undoubtedly an indication of imminent attack. The next day, the same pattern was repeated. Our U.S.-ARVN intelligence was completely accurate concerning the enemy's attack for 11 May and COMUSMACV adjusted his B-52 plan accordingly.

Early in the morning of 11 May, after several hours of intensified artillery bombardment, the enemy began his ground assault from all sides. During the fierce fighting that followed, enemy forces made extensive use of the SA-7 missile against our gunships and tactical air. They also had better coordination between tank and infantry units, but ARVN soldiers stood their ground and systematically sought to destroy enemy tanks with their proven M-72's.

As anticipated the enemy main efforts came from the west and northeast. In these areas, enemy forces succeeded in penetrating our perimeter. They seemed determined to push tanks and infantry toward the center of the city where they would link up and split our forces into enclaves. If this maneuver succeeded, the ARVN defenders would risk defeat. The situation looked bleak enough when, from their positions to the west and northeast, our forces reported they were under the threat of being overrun. The 5th Division commander reacted promptly. He sent an airborne battalion from south of the city to the endangered areas with the mission of blocking the penetrations. The effect of his move was immediate; the enemy was unable to make further progress.

In the meantime, VNAF and U.S. tactical air, which had been active since the assault began, methodically attacked enemy positions in both salients to the west and northeast. Their effectiveness was total; they not only helped contain enemy penetrations, they also inflicted heavy casualties on the entrenched enemy troops and forced some of them to abandon their positions and flee. During this day alone, nearly 300 tactical air sorties were used in support of An Loc.

The tide of the battle turned in our favor as B-52's began their strikes at 0900 hours, when the intensity of enemy tank-infantry attacks were at a peak. Thirty strikes were conducted during the next 24 hours and their devastating power was stunning. By noon, the enemy's attack had been completely broken. Fleeing in panic, enemy troops were caught in the open by our tactical air; several tank crews abandoned their vehicles. By early afternoon, no enemy tank was seen moving. Those that remained in sight were either destroyed or abandoned, several with motors still running. In one area, an entire enemy regiment which had attacked the 81st Airborne Ranger Group was effectively eliminated as a fighting force.

On 12 May, the enemy tried again but his effort was blunt and weak. A few tanks appeared but fired on the city only from standoff positions while infantry troops of both sides exchanged small arms fire around the perimeter. Despite deteriorating weather, U.S. tactical air and regular B-52 strikes continued to keep the enemy off-balance around the city. The situation was one of stalemate and contiued to be so during 13 May. Our chances of holding out in An Loc were increasing.

In the early morning of 14 May, enemy tanks and infantry attacked again from the west and southwest. This attack was broken by decisive B-52 strikes and ended by mid-morning. Taking advantage of the enemy's weakening posture, the ARVN defenders counterattacked and regained most

of the territory in the city. By now, most enemy troops had withdrawn
except for a few small blocking positions west and north of the city.
The battle had not been completely won but it was obvious that the
enemy no longer had the capability to capture An Loc.

This last attempt had cost the enemy dearly. Almost his entire
armor force committed in the battle had been destroyed. Forty of these
tanks and armored vehicles littered the battleground in and around
the city. During the following days, the situation stabilized as enemy
infantry troops completely withdrew outside the city and indirect
fire on the city continued to decrease. There were indications that the
enemy was now shifting his effort toward the 21st ARVN Division which
was moving north by road toward the besieged city.

An Loc had held against overwhelming odds. To a certain extent,
this feat could be attributed to the sheer physical endurance of ARVN
defenders and the combat audacity of such elite forces as the 81st
Airborne Ranger Group and the paratroopers. Also commendable was the
combat effectiveness of the territorial forces who fought under the
strong leadership of the province chief, Colonel Tran Van Nhut. But
the enemy's back had been broken and An Loc saved only because of timely
B-52 strikes.

Relief from the South

On 12 April, the day after An Loc was attacked for the first time,
the 21st ARVN Division closed on Lai Khe where it established a CP next
to III Corps Forward Headquarters. Its initial mission was to secure
Route QL-13 from Lai Khe to Chon Thanh, a district town 30 kilometers
due south of An Loc. The division's advance unit, the 32d Regiment,
had preceded the bulk of the division to Chon Thanh by trucks the previous
day. The mission turned out to be an usually difficult one and its
efforts encountered stiff enemy resistance from the beginning.

On 22 April, the road was blocked by the 101st NVA Regiment
(Separate) about 15 kilometers north of Lai Khe. As the 21st Division
moved north toward Chon Thanh, its advance was stopped by enemy blocking

positions. From 24 to 29 April, the division engaged the enemy in a two-pronged attack to clear the road. The 32d Regiment attacked from the north while the 33d Regiment pushed forward from the south. This pressure forced the 101st Regiment to withdraw to the west on 27 April after heavy losses, leaving behind one battalion to cover the disengagement. This battalion was finally driven from its heavily fortified positions two days later.

After clearing this road to Chon Thanh, the 21st Division initiated operations northward. It helilifted the 31st Regiment six kilometers north of Chon Thanh where this unit clashed violently for 13 days with the 165th Regiment, 7th NVA Division. During this battle, the enemy regiment sustained moderate-to-heavy losses inflicted by U.S. tactical air and B-52 strikes. It was reinforced by its sister regiment, the 209th, as the battle entered its terminal stage. On 13 May, the 31st Regiment finally overran the enemy positions. This extended the 21st Division's control of Route QL-13 to a point eight kilometers north of Chon Thanh.

Pushing northward, the division then deployed its 32d Regiment to the Tau O area five kilometers farther north. It was in this area that the hardest and longest battle was fought. The enemy was the reinforced 209th Regiment of the 7th NVA Division whose fortified blocking positions, arranged in depth, held the ARVN 32d Regiment effectively in check. I am convinced that there was no other place throughout South Vietnam where the enemy's blocking tactics were so successful as in this Tau O area. A Blocking position called "Chot", generally an A-shaped underground shelter arranged in a horseshoe configuration with multiple outlets was assigned to each company. Every three days, the platoon which manned the position was rotated so that the enemy continually enjoyed a supply of fresh troops. These positions were organized into large triangular patterns called "Kieng" (tripod) which provided mutual protection and support. The entire network was laid along the railroad, which paralleled Route QL-13, and centered on the deep swamps of the Tau O stream. This network was connected to a rubber planatation to the west by a communication trench.

Armed mostly with B-40 and B-41 rocket launchers, enemy troops from their seemingly indestructible positions stopped the 21st Division's advance for 38 consecutive days. Despite extensive use of B-52's, tactical air, and artillery, the 32d Regiment was unable to dislodge the enemy from this area. This stalemate continued until the enemy pulled out the 209th Regiment for his second attempt to capture An Loc.

Despite its failure to uproot the enemy from the Tau 0 area, the 21st Division succeeded in holding down at least two enemy regiments, making them unavailable for the attack on An Loc. In the meantime, enemy pressure on the besieged city had made relief from the outside mandatory.

One urgent requirement was to provide additional artillery support for both An Loc and the 21st Division's attack at Tau 0. To achieve this, III Corps decided to establish a strong fire support base at Tan Khai on Route QL-13, 10 kilometers south of An Loc and four kilometers north of the embattled area of Tau 0. For this effort, it employed a task force composed of the 15th Regiment, 9th ARVN Division, which had arrived from the Mekong Delta as reinforcement, and the 9th Armored Cavalry Squadron. On 15 May, one battalion of the task force began attacking north. It stayed east of Route QL-13, bypassing enemy positions. At the same time, another battalion and the task force command group made a heliborne assault into Tan Khai. The next day, the fire support base was established.

This new advance from the south soon drew the attention of the enemy. By this time, his second major effort to take An Loc had ended in failure. Shifting the effort south, on 20 May the 141st Regiment, 7th NVA Division began attacking the firebase at Tan Khai. This attack lasted for three days but the defenders of Tan Kai not only held but drove back all subsequent attacks throughout the month of June. The presence of this base, which symbolized the relief effort from the south, alleviated to some extent enemy pressure on An Loc. Although only a partial success -- Route QL-13 remained interdicted between Chon Thanh and An Loc -- the southern effort had achieved some of the effect intended. Concurrently, the defenders of An Loc fought on, both relieved and confident that in time they would prevail.

Mopping up Pockets of Enemy Resistance

As of late May, resupply by air for the besieged city became regular and efficient and the defenders were kept well supplied. This was a period of a relative lull in fighting, a respite for combat troops on the ground. Conversely, it was an ordeal for the American flyers and Vietnamese logisticians who had to struggle against great odds first to win the battle of technology and finally the battle of logistics. The fact that An Loc had held firmly to date in the face of ferocious attacks was not only because of sheer human endurance and courage on the ground and effective air support but because its defenders had been resupplied.

While the 21st Division was fighting in the Tau O area, the siege of An Loc was entering its final stage. After the second attempt to take the city and the subsequent attack on Tan Khai were unsuccessful, all three enemy divisions, the 5th, 7th and 9th, had suffered heavy casualties, estimated at about 10,000.

Taking advantage of this respite, the weary ARVN defenders within An Loc passed to the offensive with the objective of expanding the city's defense perimeter. As ARVN troops became more aggressive, they increased patrolling activities outward and began clearing the remaining enemy pockets of resistance in the northern salient. By 8 June, the 48th ARVN Regiment had eliminated all enemy resistance in this area and by 12 June, the 7th ARVN Regiment had done the same in the western part of the city.

The situation in An Loc continued to improve thereafter. On 13 and 14 June, III Corps brought in one of the 18th ARVN Division's regiments as reinforcement and fresh troops to replace the 5th Division's weary combatants. On 17 June, the 48th Regiment of the 5th Division reoccupied Hill 169. From this regained vantage point, ARVN observers were able to guide tactical air on targets of enemy troop concentration and artillery emplacements. The shelling of An Loc was greatly reduced as of that day. For the first time in several weeks, ARVN soldiers were able to loiter freely around their positions. They took a certain delight observing the destroyed enemy tanks, tangible proofs of their combat effectiveness. Above all, they enjoyed the one pleasure that had been denied them for so long: taking a bath in a nearby stream.

By 18 June, the situation had improved to the point that the III Corps commander declared that the siege of An Loc was considered terminated and released the 1st Airborne Brigade to its parent unit. And thus ended the enemy's scheme to create a capital city for the Viet Cong, and his threat on Saigon, our capital city, was eliminated.

On 7 July, President Thieu made an unannounced visit to An Loc. From a high altitude approach, his helicopter suddenly dived and landed on the soccer field. He was accompanied by Lieutenant General Nguyen Van Minh, who as III Corps commander, visited the city for the first time since it came under siege exactly three months earlier. The president was greeted by an emaciated Brigadier General Le Van Hung, the hero of An Loc, whose eyes blinked incessantly under the glaring sun. Later the president confided jokingly to an aide, "Hung looked deceitful to me. Why do you think he kept constantly squinting and blinking his eyes?" The aide replied most seriously, "Why, Mr. President, General Hung had not seen sunlight for a long, long time."

President Thieu then visited the city in ruins and the ARVN troops, to all of whom he promised promotion to the next higher rank. He also awarded General Hung with the National Order, 3d Class.

III Corps spent the remainder of the year pushing the enemy back from An Loc and rotating troops garrisoned in the city. On 11 July, the entire 18th ARVN Division closed on An Loc, replacing the 5th Division. The 25th Division also relieved the 21st Division in its incomplete mission of reducing the enemy blocking force around Tau O. Finally, the 25th Division encircled remaining enemy strongpoints and neutralized them on 20 July.

During August, the 18th Division began operations to retake the Quan Loi airfield but its efforts extended into September without success. In late November, the 18th Division was in turn replaced in An Loc by three ranger groups, the 3d, 5th and 6th which continued to secure the approaches to the city until ceasefire day.

In the meantime, the grateful people of An Loc City erected a monument dedicated to the heroic ARVN defenders. This monument stood amidst a cemetery especially built for the deceased troops of the 81st Airborne Ranger Group. The epitaph on the monument was contributed by a highly respected local elder. It read:

*"An Loc Xa Vang Danh Chien Dia
Biet Cach Du Vi Quoc Vong Than"*[3]

---

[4]Literally: Here, on the famous battleground of An Loc Town
The Airborne Rangers have sacrificed their lives
for the nation.

CHAPTER VI

Enemy Offensive in the Mekong Delta

The Setting

As major battles of the Easter Offensive began to develop in other military regions throughout South Vietnam, the Mekong Delta remained unusually quiet. But this quietness was deceptive because the enemy maintained at least six regiments within the territory of MR-4 and had the capability to reinforce with the 1st NVA Division located just across the border in Cambodia. Although the enemy's objective in MR-4 was not as clear-cut as in other military regions during the initial stage of the offensive, a very plausible theory held that he might contemplate two things. Militarily, he could try to pin down IV Corps forces, the 7th, 9th, and 21st ARVN Divisions, at home, preventing them from being redeployed to other areas. Politically, he would certainly endeavor to wreck our pacification achievements in the Mekong Delta, and by the same move, strangle its economic lifeline to the nation's capital.

In the final analysis, perhaps it was the Mekong Delta that mattered the most. The heartland of agricultural South Vietnam, it encompassed the fertile alluvial plains formed by the Mekong River and its main tributary, the Bassac. With its sixteen provinces, the Delta contained about two-thirds of the nation's population and yielded the same proportion in rice production. *(Map 15)*

The terrain of MR-4 differed radically from other regions. Flat and mostly uncovered, it consisted of mangrove swamps and ricefields crisscrossed by an interlocking system of canals, natural and artificial. Except for some isolated mountains to the west near the Cambodian border, few areas in the Delta had an elevation of more than 10 feet above sea

Map 15 — The Mekong Delta, MR-4

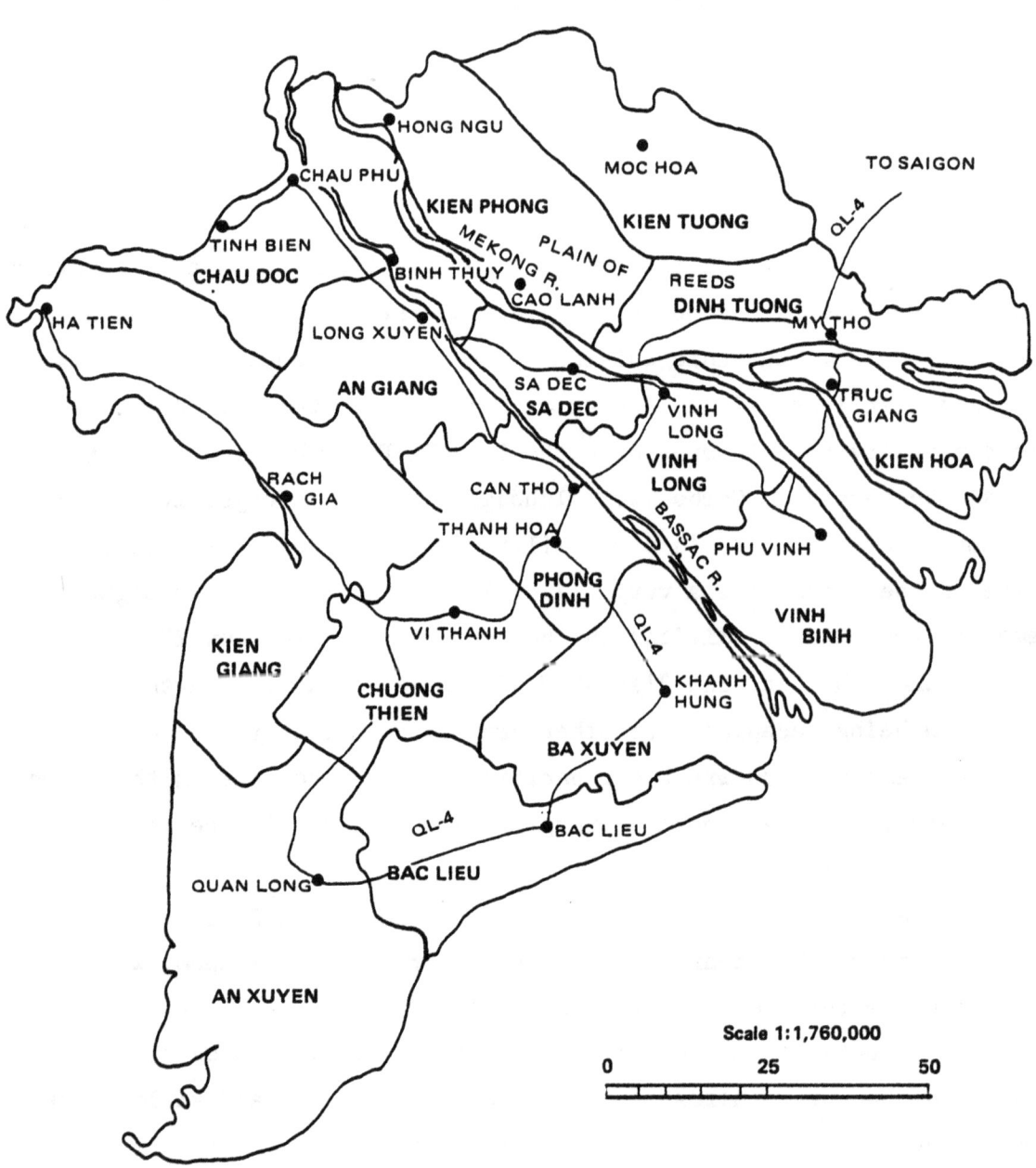

level. During the monsoon season, most of the swampy land north of Route QL-4, generally called Dong Thap Muoi (Plain of Reeds), was inundated, especially when alluvial waters raised the level of the Mekong River from July to October. Other undeveloped swampy areas along the coast had turned into havens that sheltered enemy main force units just as the scattered mini-bases inland offered good refuge for local guerrillas. *(Map 16)*

ARVN forces under the control of IV Corps consisted of three infantry divisions, two mobile and six border ranger groups. In addition, the territorial forces of MR-4 totaled about 200,000, by far the most numerous among the four military regions. The 7th ARVN Division was headquartered at Dong Tam Base in Dinh Tuong Province; the 9th Division was located in Sa Dec and the 21st Division usually operated in the Ca Mau Peninsula from its headquarters at Bac Lieu. Despite the substantial combat support and significant advisory effort, both military and civilian, provided by the United States, primary responsibility for the combat effort in MR-4 had always been Vietnamese, even during the period when U.S. units operated in the Mekong Delta.

To present a comprehensive view of the military situation throughout MR-4, it is necessary to go back to early 1970. As a result of COSVN's Resolution No. 9 disseminated in 1969, which emphasized the strategic importance of the Mekong Delta and conceived it as the principal battlefield where the outcome of the war in South Vietnam would be decided, the enemy infiltrated the 1st NVA Division Headquarters and its three regiments, the 88th, 101D and 95A into MR-4. This effort succeeded despite heavy losses. IV Corps forces were thrown off-balance and the pacification effort declined as a result of extensive enemy attacks and shellings. Not until after the enemy's sanctuaries beyond the border had been destroyed during the Cambodian incursion and his capability to resupply from the sea eliminated were these 1st NVA Division forces compelled to break down into small elements and withdraw. Part of these elements fell back into mini-bases within MR-4; others retreated toward Cambodia.

Map 16 — Enemy Base Areas in Military Region 4

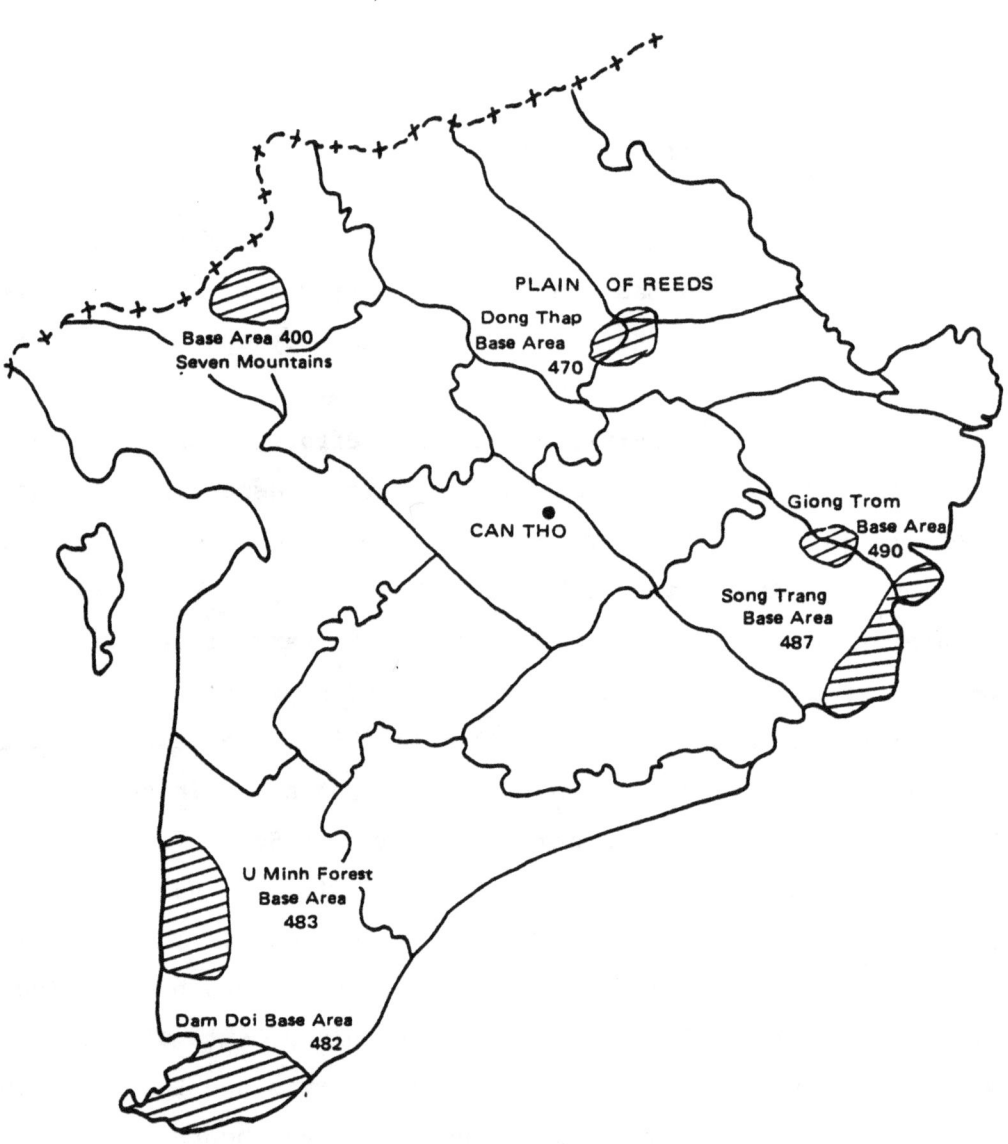

IV Corps was therefore able to regain the initiative during 1971. Its efforts during the year consisted of continuing operations on Cambodian soil to assist the weaker National Khmer Armed Forces and interdicting enemy supply routes into the Mekong Delta. Concurrently, it also emphasized the elimination of enemy's mini-bases in the Delta. This effort was crowned with resounding success as ARVN forces penetrated and destroyed most of these bases. In addition, they also established a new system of outposts to maintain GVN control over what had been the enemy's long-established base areas. The most significant achievements during this period were the neutralization of the extremely heavy enemy fortifications in the That Son (Seven Mountains) area by the 9th ARVN Division, the continued destruction of enemy installations in the U Minh Forest by the 21st ARVN Division, the coordinated activities of the 7th ARVN Division and territorial forces in Base Area 470 on the boundary of Dinh Tuong and Kien Phong Provinces, and finally, the successful pacification campaign in Kien Hoa Province, the cradle of Viet Cong insurgency.

As a result of these achievements, the situation in MR-4 was particularly bright by early 1972. About 95% of the Delta population lived in secure villages and hamlets. Rice production had increased substantially and education was available to every child of school age. Prospects for the Delta's future looked promising as key GVN programs such as Land-to-the-Tiller and Hamlet Self-Development were gaining solid momentum. The four-year Community Defense and Local Development Plan that the GVN had initiated in March 1972 presaged an even brighter future for the farmers of the Mekong Delta.

This was how the Delta looked before the enemy offensive. During the quarter that preceded it, enemy activities were at a low level, consisting mostly of small-unit attacks, harassment of outposts and scattered road interdiction. The enemy seemed to be concentrating his effort on building up supplies in his base areas, particularly in the U Minh Forest and in Dinh Tuong Province, undoubtedly preparing for future attacks. At that time, enemy forces in the Mekong Delta consited primarily of six local force regiments, all implanted in their safe havens. The 18B and 95A Regiments were in the U Minh area; the D1 and D2 Regiments were reported southwest of Chuong Thien Province; the D3 Regiment was scattered along the common boundary of Vinh Long and Vinh Binh Provinces; and the Dong Thap 1 Regiment was located in an area south of Route QL-4 in Dinh Tuong Province. Probable reinforcements from beyond the Cambodian border included the 1st NVA Division which might be introduced into Chau Doc and Kien Giang Provinces and the Z15 Regiment north of Kien Tuong Province. *(Map 17)*

During this time, the defense of the border for MR-4 was assigned to the 44th Special Tactical Zone (STZ) whose border ranger and armor forces were deployed as a screen along the Cambodian border from the Mo Vet (Parrot's Beak) area to the Gulf of Siam. In addition to its territorial defense responsibility inside MR-4, the 44th STZ also operationally controlled two major bases in Cambodia, Neak Luong, at Route QL-1 ferry crossing of the Mekong River, and Kompong Trach, some 20 km north of Ha Tien. Both bases were secured by ARVN ranger forces. The 9th ARVN Division was then conducting operations in the upper U Minh area and in Chuong Thien Province while the 21st Division operated in the lower U Minh area and in the southern portion of Cape Ca Mau. Meanwhile, the 7th ARVN Division was responsible for the two contested areas of MR-4, Dinh Tuong and Kien Hoa Provinces, and other provinces sandwiched between the Mekong and Bassac Rivers.

In mid-March, an ARVN intelligence report indicated that the entire 1st NVA Division was moving southward in Kampot Province (Cambodia), to an area deeper south than where it had been in late 1970. Two other enemy regiments, 18B and 95B, were also reported leaving the U Minh area and moving eastward in the direction of Chuong Thien Province. These movements undoubtedly presaged major actions in the Mekong Delta during the 1972 dry season.

Map 17 — Enemy Regimental Dispositions in MR-4
(01 April 1972)

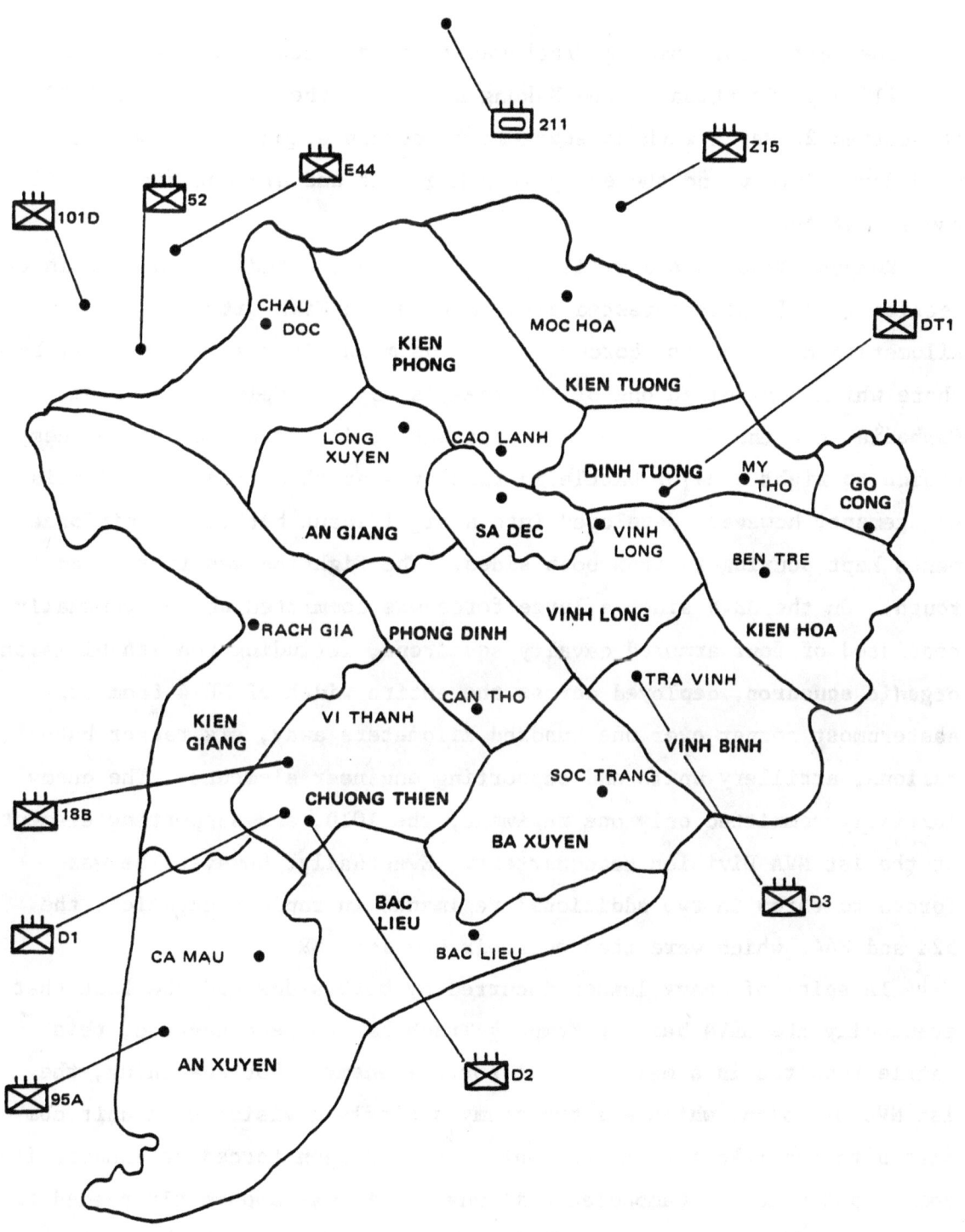

Kompong Trach: The Opening Round

The battle for Kompong Trach was to have a considerable impact on the military situation in the Mekong Delta for the remainder of 1972. It started 22 March with an engagement between elements of the 42d ARVN Ranger Group and the enemy 101D Regiment and did not abate until the end of April.

Kompong Trach was a small Cambodian town located near a road intersection in a lightly forested area north of Ha Tien City, about 15 kilometers north of the border. IV Corps maintained an operational base there which controlled one of the enemy's major supply routes from Cambodia into the Mekong Delta. Apparently, it had not been the enemy's choice to fight a major battle in this area at this time. The initial engagement, however, developed into a significant battle as reinforcements kept pouring in from both sides. The fighting was fierce and tough. On the ARVN side, a large force was committed which eventually consisted of four armored cavalry squadrons, including the 7th Division's organic squadron, deployed across the entire width of MR-4 from its easternmost corner over one hundred kilometers away, six ranger battalions, artillery units and supporting engineer elements. The enemy initially committed only one regiment, the 101D, and supporting elements of the 1st NVA Division Headquarters. Eventually, however, he was forced to throw in two additional regiments in rapid succession, the 52d and E44, which were then on their way into MR-4.

In spite of heavy losses incurred by both sides and the fact that eventually the ARVN base at Kompong Trach had to be evacuated, this battle resulted in a major defeat for the enemy. For one thing, the 1st NVA Division, which was the enemy's single division size unit committed to the Mekong Delta at that time, had been forced to exhaust its combat potential on Cambodian soil whereas it was apparently needed to conduct major actions inside MR-4 in concert with the offensive in other areas of South Vietnam. Fighting this battle, the enemy did not succeed in breaking the household china, his primary objective;

he managed only to cause minor damage to the outer fence. In other words, his mission to destroy the pacification progress in IV Corps was unsuccessful; he caused only minor disruption. Even then, the price he had to pay for it was outrageously high. The hugh losses which had been inflicted on him by our armor firepower and the devastating U.S. and VNAF airstrikes during his massive infantry assaults finally reduced the 1st NVA Division into a unit that was no longer combat worthy for the rest of the offensive.

The battle of Kompong Trach took place in an area far removed from our normal supply lines. Access by road and waterway to the battleground was limited. As a result, IV Corps had difficulty in the movement of troops and supplies for the support of the ARVN effort.[1] In fact, the battle was just an exchange of military assets and it did not involve the lives and properties of the Mekong Delta's population.

The Hau Giang Under Attack

While the battle at Kompong Trach was raging, the enemy initiated offensive activities in the Mekong Delta with a series of attacks on 7 April. Most of these attacks occurred in the province of Chuong Thien. They were conducted by four local main force units, the 18B, 95B, D1 and D2 Regiments, which almost in unison endeavored to destroy all friendly bases and outposts along the enemy's communication routes. These routes originated in the large U Minh base area, ran through the provinces of Chuong Thien and Phong Dinh, then connected the Hau Giang area (the provinces west of the Bassac River) with the Tien Giang area (the provinces east of the Mekong River).

Elsewhere in the Delta, enemy main force and local units also surfaced to put pressure on our territorial forces in an attempt to

---

[1] IV Corps Headquarters and almost all support units were located in Can Tho, the focal point of MR-4.

disrupt GVN pacification achievements. Despite the fact that these attacks were spread over a large geographical area, the enemy offensive affected only remote outposts and territorial forces, almost to the exclusion of ARVN main force units. *(Map 18)*

To help maintain tactical balance for MR-4, U.S. tactical air and B-52 strikes, which had not been used in the Delta since the beginning of 1972, resumed in support of ARVN forces at Kompong Trach and in other areas under contest throughout MR-4. This support from the air had a significant impact on the final outcome of the enemy offensive. Without it, it is doubtful that the ARVN ground forces, which fought so well at Kompong Trach, Kien Tuong, at the Elephant's Foot and in Dinh Tuoung would have been able to defeat so decisively the large enemy forces engaged in these battle areas. At best, ARVN might have been able to achieve a stalemate in some of those engagements.

On 7 April, the day enemy attacks began in MR-4, the 21st ARVN Division was ordered to prepare for movement to MR-3. Three days later, the first elements of this division were already deployed along Route QL-13 north of Lai Khe. Then, about a month later, on 12 May, another MR-4 unit, the 15th Regiment of the 9th Division, was deployed to MR-3 in the effort to relieve enemy pressure on An Loc. These redeployments resulted in big voids which would affect the defense posture of MR-4. Consequently, IV Corps had to readjust the tactical areas of responsibility over the entire border area with its mobile and border ranger units, to include a ranger group just released from its reinforcement mission in MR-1. The 9th Division (-) took over responsibility for all the provinces in the Hau Giang (Bassac) area while the 7th Division was given responsibility for the Tien Giang (Mekong) area with the majority of its effort concentrated north of Route QL-4.

In spite of the overextension of its forces and the increasingly strong pressure coming from the Cambodian border, IV Corps continued to meet the challenge effectively. Major General Nguyen Vinh Nghi, who had replaced me as IV Corps commander in early May, proved to be the man for this challenge because of his familiarity with the Mekong Delta. His actions were timely and responsive. A cautious man by

Map 18 — Enemy Attacks in MR-4

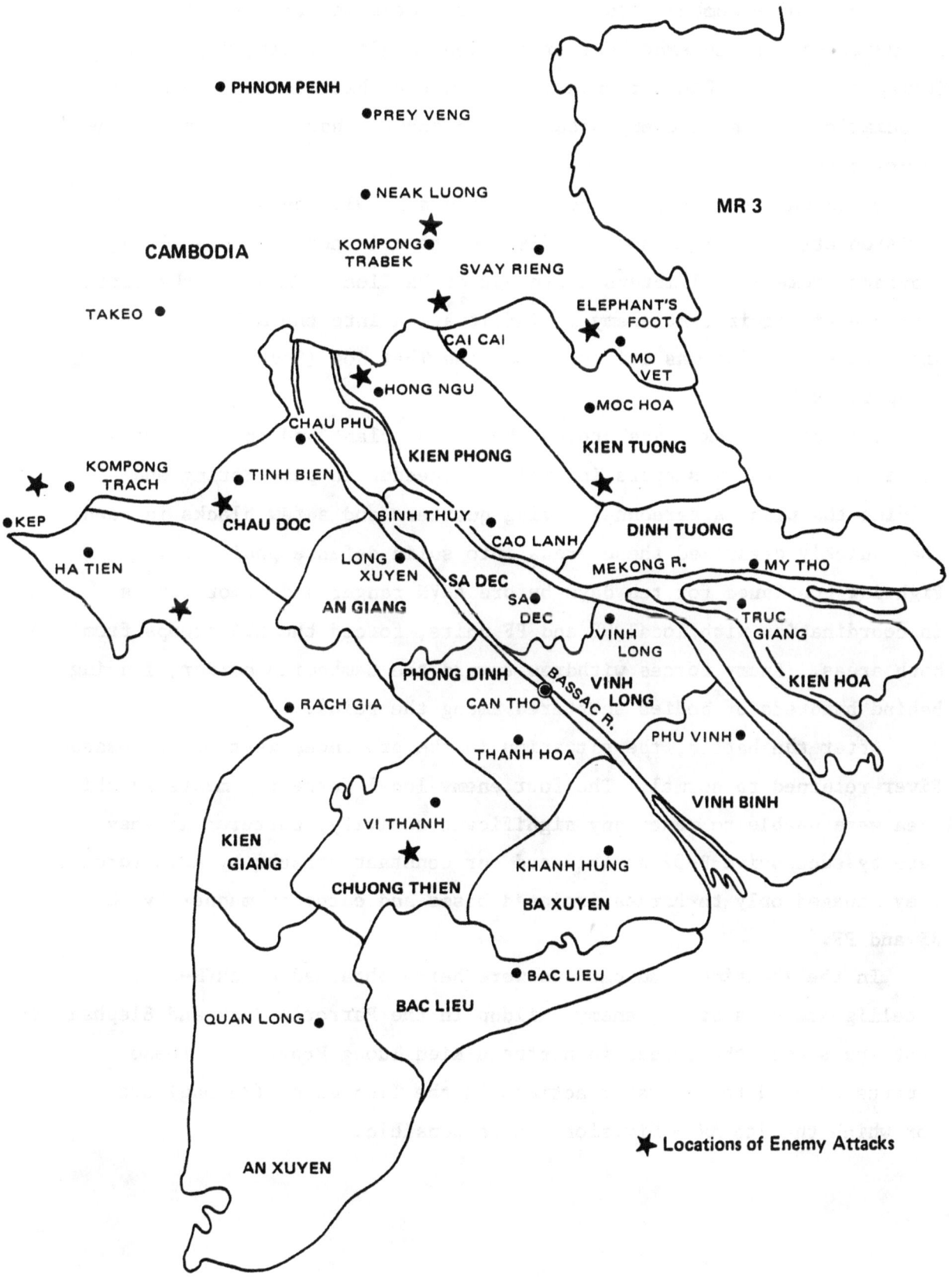

nature, he nevertheless accepted reasonable risks whenever required in order to resolve combat situations. His energetic drive and talent for maneuver left an excellent impression on his adviser, Major General Thomas M. Tarpely, DRAC commander. They worked hand in hand in close association in almost every situation to ensure that the Delta remained secure during the enemy offensive.

On 18 May, elements of the enemy 52d and 101D Regiments, 1st NVA Division attacked Kien Luong, a district town in northern Kien Giang Province, some 20 kilometers southeast of Ha Tien. This was the first instance of significant enemy re-infiltration into the Mekong Delta since this division was driven out of the That Son (Seven Mountains) area in April 1971.

The battle took place around the cement plant and in the town's market area. Enemy sappers initially succeeded in penetrating and holding the plant's personnel living quarters and a few blocks in town. They quickly organized these areas into solid defense positions. Fighting continued for ten days before ARVN ranger and armor forces, in coordination with local RF and PF units, forced the NVA troops from both areas. Enemy forces withdrew toward the Cambodian border, leaving behind hundreds of bodies scattered among the ruins.

After the battle, the situation in the provinces west of the Bassac River returned to normal. The four enemy local force regiments in this area were unable to renew any significant activity, battered as they were by successive B-52 strikes and our constant attacks by ARVN forces. They managed only to harass isolated bases and outposts manned by the RF and PF.

In the meantime, indications were being obtained by ARVN-U.S. intelligence of a strong enemy buildup in the Parrot's Beak and Elephant's Foot areas near the border in northern Kien Tuong Province. These reports pointed toward major actions in the Tien Giang (Mekong) area for which the 7th ARVN Division was responsible.

Actions in the Tien Giang

On 23 May, a small engagement took place between ARVN ranger and armor forces of the 44th STZ and the NVA 207th Regiment in an area on the Cambodian side of the border, some 15 kilometers north of Cai Cai, a district town located on the common boundary of Kien Tuong and Kien Phong Provinces near the Cambodian border.

During this battle, ARVN forces captured some enemy documents which contained plans for the infiltration of NVA units into northern Kien Tuong Province and subseuqent attacks against Moc Hoa, the provincial capital. Then on 10 June, prisoner sources disclosed that the 5th NVA Division -- which had failed in its earlier effort to take An Loc in MR-3 -- was being redeployed to the Elephant's Foot area on Cambodian territory. Eventually, this unit was to move into Base Area 470 in the Plains of Reeds.

To the IV Corps commander, who had participated in MR-3 operations during the initial stage of the siege on An Loc, it became evident that after being defeated there, the hungry enemy was trying to seek refuge in the food-rich Mekong Delta. He was determined therefore to deny the enemy this refuge. Actually, a new phase of the enemy offensive was about to begin that would involve IV Corps forces in major battles not only in the Tien Giang area but also in Cambodia.

Within 48 hours, General Nghi moved the 7th Division Headquarters and two regiments into the Elephant's Foot area north of Kien Tuong Province. Soon this division was joined by its remaining elements. At the same time, U.S. tactical air and B-52 strikes repeatedly pounded away at targets of enemy troop concentration in the area. IV Corps's quick action was timely and effective. It successfully stopped the enemy's effort to infiltrate his major units into MR-4; it also afforded IV Corps more time to consolidate the defense of Dinh Tuong Province which from all indications had been the enemy's choice for refuge and future actions.

Subsequently, several heavy engagements occurred in the Elephant's Foot area. The enemy had brought along a powerful array of antiaircraft weapons to include the heat-seeking SA-7 missile which was used for the first time in the Delta. These weapons curtailed the activities of our helicopters and observation planes and inflicted extensive damage on our aircraft but intercepted by the 7th Division forces while on the move, enemy units were surprised and suffered heavy losses. After 20 days of combat, the 7th Division was in total control of the area. Following this victory on 30 June, the division commander, Brigadier General Nguyen Khoa Nam, pushed his forces farther north. Again, his effort was crowned with resounding success.

But the enemy seemed oblivious to the serious losses he had incurred. He shifted his movement westward, pushing his regiments -- two of the 5th NVA Division and the 24th and Z18 -- deeper into the Tien Giang area toward Base Area 470 where these units were to join forces with the Z15 and Dong Thap 1 Regiments. By early July, therefore, a total of six enemy regiments were reported in northern Dinh Tuong Province, about 65 kilometers southwest of Saigon. Dinh Tuong Province was about to become the area for a major contest, and perhaps this was the primary goal of his offensive in the Mekong Delta.

In the meantime, and in conjunction with his effort to infiltrate the Tien Giang area, other NVA units, probably elements of the 9th Division, began moving toward Kompong Trabek which they took in mid-June. With the support of local Khmer Rouge units, these NVA forces were endeavoring to tighten control over Route QL-1 from the Parrot's Beak area to Neak Luong on the Mekong River. By 2 July, only two towns remained under National Khmer control in this area, Neak Luong and Svay Rieng.

Since the National Khmer forces were unable to dislodge the enemy from Kompong Trabek, a combined Khmer-ARVN operation was launched to retake this town. After 22 days of fighting, ARVN forces succeeded in freeing Kompong Trabek and clearing Route QL-1 westward after a link-up with Neak Luong. However, the enemy was determined to keep this town under his control since it was located between two of his main supply lines. Consequently, as soon as ARVN units redeployed to the Delta, NVA forces would return and occupy the town. This occurred not once but several times. Finally, enemy pressure within MR-4 became so heavy that ARVN forces could no longer afford to recapture Kompong Trabek for the benefit of their National Khmer allies. After all, their very rear, the prosperous province of Dinh Tuong, was facing a serious threat from the enemy's newly infiltrated regiments.

Attacks in Dinh Tuong

The enemy took advantage of the void left in Dinh Tuong Province by the 7th ARVN Division, which was then conducting operations in Cambodia. He launched a series of coordinated attacks against three district towns, Sam Giang, Cai Be and Cai Lay during the period from 17 May to 11 July. The attacking forces initially consisted of elements of the Dong Thap 1 and Z15 Regiments. All of these attacks were driven back by territorial forces with the strong support provided by U.S. tactical air and helicopter gunships. The enemy was finally forced to withdraw into his base area (470) to refit and recover for future actions. His losses had been heavy.

Despite initial setbacks, enemy pressure was also mounting at this time on Route QL-4, the vital supply line between the Delta's ricebowl and the nation's capital. Indications were that the enemy was bringing into the area more troops. As a result, IV Corps had to move the 7th Division back into its tactical area of responsibility, leaving behind only one regiment to form a screen along the border. By that time, the 15th Regiment, 9th ARVN Division had accomplished its mission south of An Loc and was released by MR-3 for return to MR-4. It was immediately deployed to Dinh Tuong at the same time as two ranger groups and the Ranger Command of MR-4. To defeat the enemy's effort against Route QL-4 in Dinh Tuong, B-52 strikes were concentrated on enemy bases in the Delta whenever fighting became intense and profitable targets were detected.

In mid-August, as the situation in Binh Long Province became stabilized, the 21st Division was returned to MR-4 and reassigned the responsibility for the southern Hau Giang area, its former territory.

Elements of the 9th Division which formerly operated in this area were directed to the Tien Giang area where they concentrated on Dinh Tuong. These redeployments enabled the 7th Division to devote its effort to Kien Tuong Province in the north and the border area. The 44th STZ meanwhile was assigned the responsibility for the area west of the Mekong River and south of the Cambodian border, to include the eastern part of Kien Phong Province. The 7th Division was assigned a similar area of responsibility east of the Mekong River, to include the entire province of Kien Tuong.

As a result of this influx of ARVN forces in the Tien Giang area, there was an urgent need for IV Corps to provide better command and control. General Nghi therefore established IV Corps Command Forward at Dong Tam Base and placed Brigadier General Nguyen Thanh Hoang, his deputy for operations, in charge. This rather conventional approach to command and control greatly assisted General Nghi. It facilitated the execution of two major tasks that IV Corps had assigned to its subordinate units, namely to maintain contact with the enemy and destroy his units in the Delta, and to interdict his movements of men and supplies from Cambodia into South Vietnam.

During this period of command and control restructuring, the ranger forces and 9th Division, which were occasionally reinforced with the 10th and 12th Regiments, 7th Division, fought many fierce battles in Dinh Tuong Province and in Base Area 470. In early August, the ranger forces under MR-4 Ranger Command fought a major battle in the Hau My area, west-northwest of My Tho, and completely cleared this area of the enemy. This enabled IV Corps to rebuild a system of outposts along the Thap Muoi Canal and reestablish GVN control over this area which had been subverted by the enemy since the beginning of his Easter Offensive. By the end of August, enemy activities in Dinh Tuong Province had been seriously impeded by our quick and aggressive reactions on the ground and continuous pounding from the air by U.S. tactical air and B-52's.

In late August and early September, IV Corps shifted its effort toward the That Son area in Chau Doc Province where intelligence reports strongly indicated reinfiltration by elements of the 1st NVA Division.

In a quick move, IV Corps brought its forces westward into Chau Doc and across the Cambodian border into an area west of Nui O. At the same time, it moved the 44th STZ Headquarters back to Chi Lang with the mission of engaging the 1st NVA Division, turning over the province of Kien Phong to the 7th ARVN Division.

The Aftermath

During the month of September, the situation in the Delta remained relatively uneventful. Not until early October did enemy-initiated actions resume again at a high level. The enemy's increased effort appeared to have some connection with the cease-fire agreement which was being finalized in Paris. In this effort, the 1st NVA Division sent its two regiments, the 42d and 101D, south into An Giang Province and concurrently west into the Ba Hon Mountain area near the coast in Ha Tien Province. East of the Mekong River, elements of the 207th NVA and the E2 Regiments, which were operating in the area of Kompong Trabek and north of Cai Cai, also infiltrated into Kien Phong Province. South of the Bassac River, the enemy's 18B, 95A, D1 and D2 Regiments simultaneously moved eastward, establishing blocking positions along lines of communication and among populous areas. This fanning-out pattern clearly indicated an attempt by the enemy to extend his presence over the Delta, undoubtedly in preparation for a standstill cease-fire. However, by the end of October when the cease-fire agreement failed to materialize, these activities declined significantly.

In late October and early November, the 7th ARVN Division made several contacts with the enemy in Kien Phong Province. During a battle in the Hong Ngu District where the Mekong River crossed the border, elements of the division, in coordination with territorial forces, annihilated one battalion of the 207th NVA Regiment, taking a total of 73 prisoners during eight days of engagement. This turned out to be the largest single group of enemy prisoners ever captured during the war. Most of these prisoners were teen-agers, ill-fed and ill-equipped, some without weapons or ammunition. They disclosed that they had been abandoned by their leaders who fled when the fighting became tough.

Along the common boundary of Kien Tuong and Kien Phong Provinces, the 10th Regiment, 7th ARVN Division also harvested repeated success during contacts made with infiltrated elements of the E2 Regiment, 5th NVA Division. These victories were achieved with the significant support of U.S. Army Air Cavalry teams. Finally, an enemy scheme to attack Cao Lanh, the provincial capital of Kien Phong, was preempted by the quick deployment of the 11th and 12th Regiments, 7th Division into this area.

Meanwhile, farther west of the Bassac River, ranger forces of the 44th STZ conducted successful operations in Ha Tien Province and the That Son area. During these operations, they captured several supply caches, destroyed enemy installations and inflicted substantial losses to elements of two NVA regiments, the 52d and 101D of the 1st Division. A battalion commander of the 52d NVA Regiment surrendered to the rangers and he disclosed that his battalion had been so severely mauled by our ambushes and airstrikes that only 30 men were left.

As of mid-December, the overall situation in the Mekong Delta returned to its pre-offensive quietness. IV Corps took advantage of this respite to readjust command and control, expanding the 7th Division's TAOR to include both Dinh Tuong and Go Cong Provinces as the first step. The 9th Division was then assigned responsibility for the provinces of Sa Dec, Vinh Long, Vinh Binh and Kien Hoa. This extension of ARVN forces brought about an improvement in territorial security, especially in those areas where enemy pressure was heavy and our territorial forces needed ARVN support.

This quiet period lasted only for about two weeks through Christmas and New Year's day. After that, enemy-initiated activities resumed at a fairly high level. However, despite their increased frequency, most of these activities were low-keyed and inconsequential. It was obvious then that the October pattern was repeating itself and the enemy was apparently more concerned with his omni-presence as a psychological and political ploy to influence the local population and stimulate the morale of his own troops than trying to obtain military gains. This was the situation throughout the Mekong Delta on the eve of the cease-fire. *(Map 19)*

In summary, in spite of his multiple efforts and heavy sacrifices during the Easter Offensive, the enemy accomplished very little in the Mekong Delta. Route QL-4, which was one among the enemy's major objectives, remained open throughout his offensive save for brief periods of traffic interruption. He had failed to strangle our vital lifeline; he had also failed to disrupt our pacification effort. No district town, not even the remotest, be it in Kien Hoa, Ca Mau or along the border, ever fell into enemy hands, even temporarily. Despite some ups and downs in the pacification effort, the enemy was unable to achieve any additional gains in population control. And most remarkably, all our lines of communication, roads or waterways, remained trafficable throughout his offensive.

On their part, the ARVN forces of MR-4 had performed remarkably well. They had effectively prevented the enemy from achieving big gains and had finally defeated him soundly, this despite their initial failure to prevent further infiltration. The accomplishments of the 7th and 9th Divisions, the rangers, and the RF and PF in the Mekong Delta, although not as dramatic as the combat exploits achieved in heroic An Loc, proud Kontum or victorious Tri-Thien, certainly did have a decisive impact on the survival of South Vietnam. Our strategists had always emphasized that, "He who won the battles in the Mekong Delta would win the war in South Vietnam" Not only had IV Corps won the battles in the Mekong Delta but it had done this while sharing nearly one half of its forces with MR-3 and MR-1.

Map 19 — Enemy Regimental Dispositions in MR-4 - (31 December 1972)

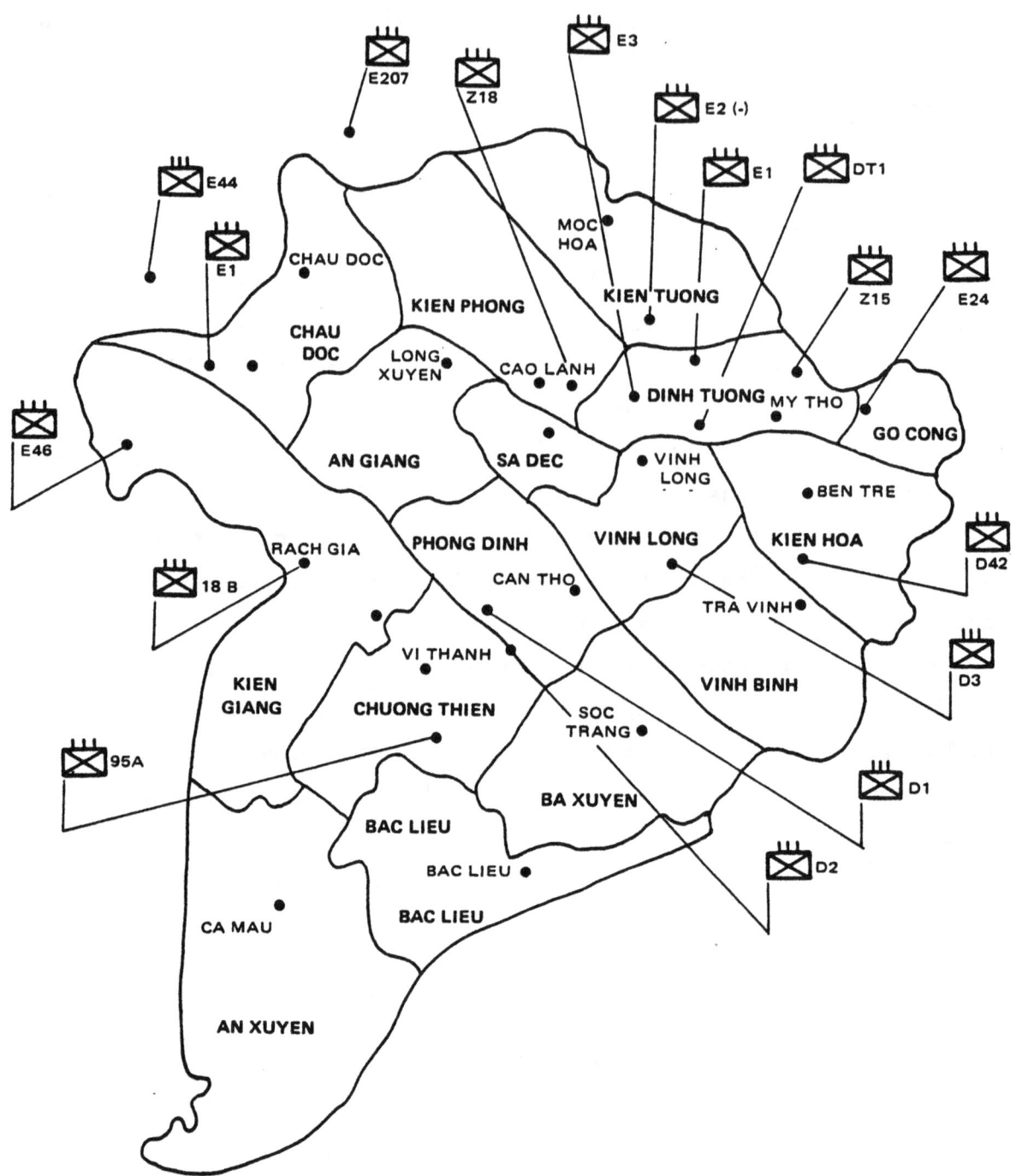

CHAPTER VII

A Critical Analysis

North Vietnam's Objectives, Strategy, and Tactics

Since their major defeats during 1968 and 1969, the Communist leaders in Hanoi had the urgent requirement to accomplish two things. First, they needed to improve their deteriorating strategic posture in South Vietnam, and second, to have an ultimate chance to win, they had to defeat the vietnamization process. Politically, as Viet Cong negotiators later disclosed in Paris, North Vietnam's leaders also strongly believed they needed a leverage to strengthen their demand for a coalition government in the South. To obtain this leverage, it was mandatory that they control through military action as much territory of the Republic of Vietnam as possible. This was the rationale behind North Vietnam's decision, made in mid-1971, to conduct the 1972 invasion.

Hanoi's campaign plans for 1972 reflected a change in strategy. To hasten and force a solution to the war of their own choice on the United States and South Vietnam, its leaders were prepared to short-circuit the evolutionary phases of a protracted war of liberation and take the calculated risks of a decisive, all-out offensive.

One of the most revealing indications of North Vietnam's new strategic approach appeared in an unnumbered resolution adopted by its Central Office for South Vietnam in December 1971. In its own conceptual words, this resolution called for "tilting the balance of forces through the use of main-force warfare and political initiative." In more down-to-earth terms, it advocated defeating vietnamization and pacification, expanding the territory under Viet Cong control, and protecting base areas and lines of communication in Laos, Cambodia, and South Vietnam.

Additional revelations of the enemy's objectives were also obtained throughout the last six months of 1971 from captured documents and agent reports. Finally, these objectives were found summarized in COSVN Directive No. 43, dated March 1972. Basically, this directive reiterated and elaborated on the major objectives already outlined in the unnumbered resolution of December 1971. But it also disclosed other objectives that COSVN was concurrently contemplating, namely, disrupting the RVN economy, improving the morale of the Viet Cong Infrastructure (VCI), influencing American and world opinion, and discrediting and overthrowing the Thieu administration.

North Vietnam's principal goal for 1972, inferred from these objectives, seemed to be a standstill cease-fire as soon as it had achieved some territorial gains. From this improved bargaining position, our enemy felt certain he could force negotiators into accepting a solution to the war that would be most favorable for his side.

The Nguyen Hue campaign failed to accomplish intended objectives. In exchange for some insignificant territorial gains, North Vietnam had virtually exhausted its manpower and materiel resources. Estimates placed its losses at over 100,000 casualties and at least one half of its large-caliber artillery and tanks. By the end of 1972, it became obvious that Hanoi no longer possessed the capabilities for another general offensive in South Vietnam in the immediate future. At the price of this huge sacrifice, the gains that North Vietnam had achieved looked insignificant indeed. Not one of the 44 provincial capitals of South Vietnam -- with the exception of the temporary occupation of Quang Tri -- ever fell into enemy hands. Out of the 260 district towns, fewer than ten were occupied, almost all of them located in remote border areas, far removed from centers of population. What then caused North Vietnam's failure to attain its military and political objectives?

It was obvious that when planning the Easter invasion, North Vietnam's leaders had grossly underestimated two things: first, the RVNAF capability for sustained combat and capacity for endurance, especially as far as the territorial forces were concerned; and second, the extent and effectiveness of U.S. airpower. In addition, their ill-fated offensive was conducted with several apparent strategic and tactical miscalculations.

In the first place, Hanoi made a basic strategic error when it dispersed its main force units and made major efforts on three widely separated fronts instead of concentrating them in a major thrust against a single objective. Although he was successful in gaining some territory in each region under attack, only in northern Quang Tri Province did these gains have much political or military significance. Had he, on the other hand, concentrated on one main effort, he might have succeeded in occupying more terrain of greater value at less cost.

At the beginning of the offensive, Hanoi rejoiced as NVA forces attacked vigorously across the DMZ, pushed beyond Dong Ha, occupied Quang Tri City and appeared to have a clear access to Hue. If the invading forces immediately following their capture of Quang Tri City could have continued the drive south and southeast with one or two divisions that were being committed in other areas of South Vietnam, Hanoi would certainly have been able to maintain the momentum. Hue City could have fallen to such a concentrated effort and this would have had a major impact throughout South Vietnam. But Hanoi failed to exploit its initial success. By spreading its forces, it lost this capability. Kontum and An Loc might also have been more vulnerable to the enemy if the initial momentum had been sustained. Hanoi was too proud to admit that its forces were anything less than invincible and did not believe that ARVN units would be able to hold in the face of his offensive and its superiority in tanks and artillery.

Apparently, Hanoi also failed to realize in advance that its divergent attacks and timing would enable South Vietnam to commit additional forces into the battles and make up for initial disadvantages. Lack of enemy momentum also contributed to the RVN having enough time to rearrange the deployment of its combat units. The JGS was thus able to assemble the entire Airborne Division, which was then attached piecemeal to Military Region 2 and Military Region 3, move it to northern Military Region 1 and then redeploy other ARVN units to Kontum and the An Loc area. All redeployments were made in time for the key battles that decided the fate of these contested areas. So instead of losing one ARVN unit after another as might have happened if the invasion of Quang Tri had been exploited with additional NVA divisions, South Vietnam was able to deploy its divisions into the three fronts, overcoming North Vietnam's initial advantage.

Hanoi's strategic error was further compounded by tactical blunders; two such blunders were most obvious. First, it appeared that all NVA tactical commanders lacked experience in the employment of armor. After overcoming the many problems of introducing tanks into South Vietnam successfully, they failed to use them properly. Instead of making deep thrusts into our lines, creating shock and confusion and disrupting our rear areas, they employed them with hesitancy, primarily in attacks against targets whose armor defenses had been carefully prepared. Our forces learned that some armor vehicles, especially those with external fuel tanks, could be put out of action even by artillery shell fragments.

The second most remarkable tactical error derived from their own concept of infantry assaults. Having initial numerical advantage in all of the major areas of contest, they squandered it in suicidal, massive assaults whose attrition rate was so great that replacements could not possibly maintain unit strengths. This was true despite the fact that they usually had a good replacement capability. The continued attrition gradually shifted the balance to our advantage. Several NVA battalions were so badly mauled that they were reduced to less than fifty personnel. During the final stage of the offensive, the deterioration of NVA strength and morale was such that desertion became a serious problem for front line units. Some entire units broke contact hastily and retreated, leaving equipment behind. Such events had rarely happened when we engaged NVA units prior to this time.

The Defense Posture of South Vietnam

North Vietnam thus committed several major strategic and tactical errors during its Easter invasion and these errors contributed to its

Captured NVA T-54 Tank Displayed in Saigon, 14 May 1972

Public Display of NVA Weapons Captured During 1972 Easter Offensive

eventual failure. However, during the offensive's initial stage, the enemy had the upper hand, advancing from victory to victory on all three fronts. His initial success derived not so much from superior strength or firepower, than from the weaknesses of our defense posture. Not only was South Vietnam's geographical position one of its major vulnerabilities, but the organization and disposition of South Vietnam's defense forces were not adequate for the early containment of an enemy invasion of such proportions.

In spite of their ultimate failure, the fact should be admitted that during the initial stage of the invasion, NVA forces were almost invincible wherever they attacked. They succeeded in occupying Quang Tri in Military Region 1, Dakto in Military Region 2 and Loc Ninh in Military Region 3 with relative rapidity and ARVN defenses crumbled in the face of advancing NVA tanks and infantry. However, the 3d, 22d, and 5th ARVN Divisions were all considered combat ready and had been fully prepared and alerted for major enemy attacks. What caused these early defeats? Looking back on our defense posture at that time, I personally believe that South Vietnam could have done little to prevent these initial setbacks.

In the first place, the geographical configuration of South Vietnam did not lend itself to defense against an invasion. From the DMZ to Cape Ca Mau, South Vietnam was a narrow strip of land averaging approximately one hundred miles in width; at one place, less than 50 miles. But the narrowness would not have been a problem if South Vietnam had been a peninsula surrounded by waters like South Korea. Unfortunately, South Vietnam's western border from the DMZ to Ha Tien City was over 600 miles long. About two thirds of it ran through the jungles and mountains along the Laotian and Cambodian borders, and the southern 200 miles through relatively flat terrain consisting mostly of scrub forests, swamps, and rice farmland. This open border area did not provide the natural features needed for an effective defense. Furthermore, it was especially difficult to defend against an enemy who enjoyed total freedom of movement along the entire frontier. Because of the exposure of this western flank, the enemy was able to infiltrate and build up his forces with little interruption and attack where and when he wished.

As a result, any determined enemy attack could be driven a considerable distance into South Vietnam's territory before adequate forces could be deployed to contain it. In the face of this vulnerability, South Vietnam was compelled to deploy its forces in a manner as to be able to monitor the entire length of the western border. Our forces were therefore thinly deployed at firebases and border camps from the DMZ to the U Minh Forest. Not only could the enemy usually overrun any of the border outposts with a determined attack, but this disposition also immobilized a sizeable force; when enemy attacks materialized in several places at the same time, it was impossible to commit reserves until we could determine where the enemy would make his main effort. South Vietnam was thus forced into a difficult defensive posture which did not offer its forces adequate tactical flexibility and the enemy always enjoyed a definite advantage wherever he chose to attack.

Obviously, South Vietnam became even more difficult to defend when U.S. and Free World Military Assistance (FWMA) forces were withdrawn. Our divisions found themselves overextended almost to the breaking point in order to fill the areas vacated by our departing allies. Because of this overextension, our South Vietnamese divisions lost even more flexibility. In the meantime, NVA forces located in South Vietnam were growing with every passing year. From 149 combat battalions at the end of 1969 when U.S. forces began to redeploy, NVA forces almost doubled to a total of 285 battalions by the end of 1972. These forces were also becoming more conventional in organization and equipment.

If an analysis were made of the balance of forces and the relationship of capabilities between the warring parties it was evident that over the years, each party had evolved into a sizeable military force. By 1964, the ranks of original Viet Cong insurgents had been depleted to the point that they had to be replenished by North Vietnamese regulars. Then during the period from 1965 to 1972, the enemy strengthened his forces by upgrading guerrilla and local force units into main force units and increased their sizes, not with locally-recruited manpower but with entire regular units infiltrated from North Vietnam. This trend turned insurgents into aggressors and the Communist war effort in South Vietnam increasingly took on the conventional character of overt aggression. Finally, this aggression materialized during the 1972 all-out invasion.

During this same period of time the defending forces of South Vietnam, RVN, U.S. and FWMA forces, which initially had a total strength greater than our enemy's, gradually decreased. The RVN was well aware of its weakening defense posture but there was nothing it could do to strengthen this posture without additional combat forces which meant more equipment, more expenditures. It wanted to activate more divisions, more general reserve forces, but military aid was a limitation. Forced therefore to fill in the vacuum created in Military Region 1 by 80,000 departing U.S. troops, the RVN activated the 3d Division with an initial strength of less than 10,000, formed of existing elements taken here and there from other divisions. The 3d was the only division sized addition to the RVN force structure provided by the Vietnamization program.

Much unduly harsh and unjustified criticism has been directed against the performance of the 3d ARVN Division during the Easter Offensive. The division was new and untested and was deployed to a critical, potentially vulnerable area. But it was never proven that the 3d Division consisted mostly of deserters, pardoned military criminals and other undesirable elements cast off by other units. The 3d ARVN Division was no weakling. It was new only in name, not in combat experience. Five out of its nine organic infantry battalions and its armored cavalry squadron were all units with long combat records, having fought NVA forces in the DMZ area for several years. Its other four infantry battalions were transferred as complete units, not piecemeal, from ARVN and territorial forces of Military Region 1. The great majority of the troops and cadres consisted of local servicemen who were well familiar with the rugged terrain of Military Region 1 and hardened to the cold and wet climate in this part of the country. The division's staff, whose nucleus was the former forward command element of the 1st ARVN Division at Dong Ha, was well versed with operations and knew the enemy in the DMZ area. In addition, a substantial number of divisional unit commanders were those who had operated in this area, hand in hand with U.S. units and on almost every battlefield, for several years. As such, the 3d Division was anything but a green unit, although it lacked the cohesiveness and efficiency of a division that had fought together as a unit.

What then caused the demise of this division? To put it briefly, the 3d Division failed because it was overburdened. For the defense of the DMZ area, this unit had taken over the combat responsibilities formerly assigned to nearly two U.S. divisions, the reinforced U.S. 3d Marine Division and the 1/5 Brigade (Mechanized). The 3d Division was required to replace these United States units with just four infantry battalions. How could such a defense hold in the face of the strongest, concentrated enemy offensive of the war?

Some observers have suggested that another ARVN division, one that had long been established, could have done better than the 3d Division. I don't think so. I am not sure that replacing it with any other division would have been a wise move or would have changed the results. If a critic was really knowledgeable about ARVN infantry divisions and the way they had been conditioned for so many years to territorial security-related tasks, he would have realized that South Vietnam did not have much of a choice. Theoretically of course, any ARVN division was interchangeable with any other and should be able to operate anywhere in South Vietnam. In practice, however, there were only a few units capable of operating effectively in any given area across the country. Most ARVN divisions usually confined their activities and combat operations to a well-defined area of responsibility within a military region. Each became accustomed to its area and could not perform with the same effectiveness in another. If emergencies arose, any ARVN division could be employed in mobile operations far removed from its territory, but local security and pacification support requirements always compelled its deployment back to its former area of responsibility after a short time.

The 21st ARVN Division was a case in point. An old horse having ploughed the furrows of the Mekong Delta since it was born, this division was thoroughly at home in its habitat of swamps and canals where it always gave its best performance. It was much less effective in the jungles of Binh Long Province when moved into Military Region 3 to assist in the relief of An Loc. At the beginning of the offensive, there had been a plan to deploy the 21st Division to Military Region 1 as reinforcement for the Quang Tri front. At that time neither the division commander nor any other military authorities believed it would have a chance on such an unfamiliar battleground, especially when the Delta troops had never been exposed to the enemy's heavy artillery.

In addition to the problem of unfamiliarity with the new environment, there was also the complicated and unresolved problem of military dependents. This was a handicap for most ARVN divisions since their troops always grew restless after being separated from their families. If the separation was too long, some would resort to desertion. But it would not do any good to move military dependents to where the men were deployed; they preferred to live near their native towns or villages where they could rely on parents and relatives for help in eking out a living. Very few wanted to be uprooted and transplanted into a strange environment, much less to such areas as Quang Tri Province where the land was so poor that "dogs ate pebbles and chicken fed on salt," and where they would face the constant hazards of enemy shellings and inclement weather.[1]

Looking back on the ordeal of the 3d ARVN Division, I believe that not very many ARVN divisions could have held initially against the concentrated and conventional attacks launched by the enemy. I also believe that no other unit could have done anything better under the complicated command and control system which was established by the I Corps Commander.

---

[1] A statement often made by the local population of Quang Tri Province.

At the very least, however, the 3d Division did make two important contributions during the 1972 offensive. It held the Dong Ha line for a month against the overwhelming pressure of superior NVA forces, gaining enough time for Saigon to make necessary preparations for the deployment of general reserve forces to decisive battle areas. And after recovery, which took less than three months, this same division displayed remarkable combat effectiveness battling the NVA 711th Division west of Da Nang during the final stages of the 1972 enemy offensive.

RVNAF Performance

In 1972, although a few U.S. combat units were still in Vietnam, they were all committed to the defense and security of U.S. bases and installations; the RVNAF had assumed the primary responsibility for the ground war. The Americans provided advice, logistics and combat support. When the enemy offensive began, Vietnam's fate was in its own hands. President Thieu, the Joint General Staff and the corps commanders had to decide where, when and how to fight. The test of Vietnamization had come and the United States would share in its outcome.

There was no change in strategy; the concept of securing all national territory continued to be the order of the day. Every area, every strongpoint, no matter how small or remote, had to be held "at all cost." The national leadership asserted its firm determination to resist aggression and protect the integrity of South Vietnam's sovereignty; it announced that "we would not yield even a pebble in Quang Tri or a handful of mud in Ca Mau to the enemy."[2] Obviously, this declaration did not take into full account either South Vietnam's defense posture or RVNAF capabilities. A more pragmatic leader would have recognized that the RVNAF simply did not have the resources

---

[2] President Thieu's statement, reiterated many times during his 1972 visits to MR-1.

to carry out such a policy, at least not without the full support of U.S. and FWMA combat forces as in years past.

The early disaster in I Corps -- particularly the decimation of the 3d Division -- can be attributed largely to the failure of the corps commander and his staff to provide adequate guidance and support to this front-line division. It was the customary practice at I Corps headquarters to shift all tactical responsibility to the divisions, simply by repeating verbatim -- perhaps with a few words added -- the general mission guidance received from Saigon, such as "Quang Tri must be held at all costs." It did not matter that the division was ill-equipped or too meagerly supported to accomplish such a mission. If Saigon said that a place must be held at all costs, the fact that the corps repeated these instructions to the division was enough to place all responsibility for execution upon the division commander. No one would later question whether the mission was feasible or whether the operation was well supported by the corps. In I Corps, the commander believed that he had done his job when he had said, pointing to a map, "attack there," or "defend here at all costs." When the 3d Division failed, this logic dictated that its commander be tried for its failure, convicted, and sent to prison.

During the initial stage of the offensive, South Vietnamese military authorities reacted just as they had during past periods of increased activity. All deployments and reinforcements were continued in the same piecemeal, fractional manner, a brigade here, a battalion there. The initial efforts were indecisive and not enough to regain the initiative. And when these fragmentary reinforcements accumulated in one area, they created difficult command and control problems with the result that units were not employed with maximum effectiveness.

Quang Tri was an excellent example. It showed that our systems for command and control and our techniques of employment of forces were not adequate to counter the conventional, combined-arms tactics being used by the NVA. While NVA forces used artillery to the maximum of its capability, our artillery was seldom placed under centralized control. In almost every case, firing batteries were fragmented into elements and implanted in fixed positions. As a result, the full effect of massed artillery fire was rarely achieved by an ARVN division. Against massed tank and infantry formations, our dispersed artillery was unable to concentrate enough destructive fire to disrupt them. This not only happened at Quang Tri during the initial battles but, unfortuantely, persisted to a somewhat lesser degree throughout the offensive. Commanders failed to coordinate properly all of the usually abundant fires that were available at division level. There included U.S. naval gunfire and tactical air, and Vietnamese tactical air and artillery.

After the initial setbacks, however, the national leadership undertook to remedy some of these errors and shortcomings, to include the replacement of certain key commanders in the field. Consequently, the employment of combat and combat support units in combined-arms operations improved significantly. Procedures for the coordinated use of air, naval gunfire and artillery were also developed. The result was that ARVN units, which consisted of courageous and resilient soldiers, were eventually able to stand firm and defeat NVA attacks.

When the enemy launched his Nguyen Hue offensive, I am certain that he expected to quickly seize some of his major objectives. However, he was unsuccessful. An Loc held firm; so did Kontum, and Quang Tri was eventually retaken. Obviously, he did not believe that the RVNAF could recover so quickly after initial reverses. This capability became characteristic of RVNAF maturity and combat effectiveness. The enemy also learned that the RVNAF, with adequate U.S. support, was capable of resisting the best efforts of North Vietnamese Army.

At An Loc the super-human endurance and resourcefulness of ARVN troops helped reverse the trend of several battles and the decisive B-52 strikes finally broke the enemy siege. Although this was definitely a victory for the RVNAF, a victory achieved at high cost in men and equipment, the III Corps counteroffensive stalled at the end of the year, with the enemy still in control of most of the areas he had occupied during the initial stage of the offensive. The RVNAF simply lacked the capability to mass the force required to open Route 13 past Chon Thanh or past An Loc into Loc Ninh.

In Kontum, the enemy fought desperate battles with apparent disregard for casualties; he lost over 4,000 men there. He had succeeded in capturing part of the city but could not hold it beyond mid-June when the 23d ARVN Division regained control. II Corps' painful effort to clear Route QL-14 from Pleiku to Kontum terminated in early July when this road was reopened to commercial traffic, although enemy interdictions continued periodically until year's end. ARVN operations conducted north of Kontum to regain control of the lost territory were not as successful. Until cease-fire day, the enemy was still in control of the area north of the city, from Vo Dinh to Dak Pek. As in Military Region III, the forces that would be needed to carry a counter offensive north into strongly defended enemy bases were not available.

The RVNAF counteroffensive in Military Region 1 was by far the most vigorous effort to retake lost territory and was partially successful. Quang Tri City was recaptured but only after 80 long days of bloody fighting. By the time the marines regained control of the old citadel in mid-September, the city was smoldering ruins. At year's end, the RVNAF marines pushed north along the coast until they reached the Thach Han River's estuary. I Corps's farthest offensive spearhead to the west, meanwhile, terminated when ARVN paratroopers retook FSB Anne. The defense of Hue City also became more consolidated as the 1st ARVN Division successfully pushed westward to the vicinity of FSB Veghel. But we were unable to restore the old frontier along the DMZ.

U.S. Support

One of the major factors contributing to the RVNAF success in stalling and eventually defeating the enemy's Easter Offensive was United States support. Never before had the American response to the NVA threat been so forceful and determined. Among other things, the United States substnatially increased its air and naval fire support and provided South Vietnam with as much equipment and supplies as was required. Furthermore, this support was coordinated with an increased bombing campaign in South Vietnam, increased interdiction of enemy supply lines in Laos, renewed bombing of North Vietnam and the blockade of major North Vietnamese ports, all in a remarkably successful effort to reduce the effect of the enemy offensive.

The role of the U.S. Air Force was decisive in several instances. The support provided by U.S. tactical air and B-52's on all major fronts was timely and most effective; it not only destroyed many enemy formations but also sustained the morale of the ARVN soldiers. If laudatory words are used here to describe the U.S. Air Force's contributions to the RVNAF success in repelling the enemy's biggest offensive to date, they certainly should not be construed as flattery; they only serve to convey due credit for a highly professional performance. Quang Tri City certainly could not have been retaken, nor could ARVN forces have held at Kontum and An Loc, had it not been for the support provided by the U.S. Air Force.

Strategic air was also a vital and decisive factor contributing to RVNAF success. In Military Region 1, for instance, there was absolutely no way for the Airborne and the Marine Divisions to resist the ferocious attacks by five reinforced and strongly supported NVA divisions without the support of B-52's. Not only did B-52 strikes damage enemy support activities, they also provided excellent close support. An Loc and Kontum would have been in serious jeopardy if B-52 strikes had not been planned to destroy assaulting masses of enemy infantry and armor. The MACV J2 and J3 did a splendid job in planning this timely and effective support.

The only adverse effect that can be attributed to the employment of B-52's was that in time, ARVN forces may have become too dependent on them. Since U.S. air support was so effective and always available, ARVN tactical commanders tended to disregard their own supporting weapons which were seldom used properly. Eventually the tendency to rely on B-52's or tactical air in the place of organic fires and maneuver became so commonplace that it inhibited initiative and often caused delays in conducting attacks. In several instances, ARVN units marked time on the line of departure because they were convinced that their attack would not be successful until B-52's dropped their loads. This tendency was a major handicap for the RVNAF during the post-ceasefire period when B-52s and U.S. air support were no longer provided.

In addition to firepower, the American effort to provide adequate logistic support contributed immeasurably to the RVNAF success. As a result of repeated setbacks during the initial stage of the offensive, some ARVN units incurred unusually heavy losses in materiel. To help the RVNAF replace materiel losses and fight effectively against modern weapon systems introduced by the Communist Bloc, the United States initiated immediate action to provide the RVNAF with whatever equipment was required for their combat needs. Without this timely support, the RVNAF would not have been able to survive the enemy's sustained attacks. Our support requirements were unusually large, especially in artillery pieces, armored vehicles, trucks and signal equipment, and caused a substantial drain on the U.S. logistic system. The high expenditure of ammunition by ARVN units during this offensive also posed special supply problems that only the vast American logistic system could solve efficiently.

Throughout the enemy offensive, the American advisory effort also contributed significantly to the RVNAF success; it was more productive than it had ever been. The advisory effort had been gradually expanded as the combat role of U.S. forces in South Vietnam phased down. At the corps level, since the advent of regional assistance commands, corps senior advisers were able to devote all their time and energy to advising and assisting their counterparts. The role of U.S. advisers encompassed a vast scope of activities. In assisting the ARVN commander, the U.S. adviser helped him detect and identify problem areas, establish priorities in solving them, and organize the means and resources needed to accomplis- his tasks.

By the time the NVA offensive was initiated in 1972, a great number of advisers at battalion level had been withdrawn and regimental advisers were also reduced accordingly. Because of the intensity of the fighting, however, MACV deemed it necessary to reinstate advisers for some ARVN units where their presence was critically needed (these advisers were withdrawn as soon as the RVNAF regained the initiative.) As a result, advisers found themselves once again participating in daily combat operations during the Easter Offensive, working hand in hand with ARVN counterparts and sharing in their success or failure.

Despite the American policy which dictated that advisers were to remain with their units regardless of enemy pressure, the regional senior advisers was empowered to extricate them from immediate dangers. There were a few instances during the offensive when advisers had to leave their units. Most of them, however, welcomed the challenge of staying with their counterparts until the very last minute to provide moral support and coordinate the employment of tactical air and gunships for their embattled units.

At the corps and division levels, advisers played a most significant role. They assisted corps and division staffs in planning and supervising combat operations and developing procedures for the effective use and coordination of tactical air, naval gunfire and artillery. These were the areas in which ARNV commanders and their staffs most required assistance. The regional assistance commands, therefore, proved to be timely and most responsive institutions that greatly assisted the ARVN Corps during the 1972 Easter Offensive.

CHAPTER VIII

Summary and Conclusions

Prior to the invasion of 1972, Hanoi had launched several large-scale offensive campaigns in South Vietnam, such as the 1968 "General Offensive - General Uprising" which included the siege on Khe Sanh Base, all with the commitment of multi-division forces. But none of these initiatives equaled the 1972 Easter Offensive -- or the Nguyen Hue Campaign as the enemy called it -- in scale and in importance. Undoubtedly, Hanoi had intended it to be a decisive military effort.

The importance and decisiveness of this effort were readily apparent by the forces Hanoi had committed -- at least ten infantry divisions and hundreds of tanks and artillery pieces. The Hanoi leadership always timed its major efforts to exert maximum impact on American domestic politics. The 1972 Easter Offensive was in line with this policy. And true to their doctrinal precepts, the Communist leaders of North Vietnam evidenced little concern for personnel and equipment losses, provided that the ultimate objectives set forth by their Politbureau could be attained.

From its very beginning, this offensive was an ultimate challenge for South Vietnam. At various times in some geographical areas, victory appeared to be within reach of the enemy. Indeed, the initial stage of Hanoi's offensive had been successful beyond the capability of its forces to exploit. In northern Military Region 1, NVA units had in rapid succession taken one firebase after another in the DMZ area -- 14 in all -- with little resistance from ARVN forces. In Military Region 3, three of Hanoi's divisions rapidly overwhelmed ARVN forces and seized Loc Ninh. In this area alone, they annihilated two ARVN regiments and laid siege to An Loc. In the Central Highlands, two other NVA divisions overran Dakto-Tan Canh and a series of firebases on Rocket Ridge overlooking Kontum City. The initial mouentum of the NVA offensive was awesome.

After these unexpectedly easy victories, NVA forces concentrated their attacks during late April on Quang Tri City, captured this provincial capital and advanced toward Hue. This ancient city of great political importance was in grave danger. By mid-May, NVA forces in Military Region 2 were in position to slash across the width of South Vietnam from Kontum to Binh Dinh. Additionally, by the middle of May in Military Region 3, the enemy had seized a portion of An Loc just one hundred kilometers north of Saigon. NVA forces were also in control of several large, though remote areas which local governments had evacuated. However, the RVNAF consolidated its defense and stalled the momentum of the enemy invasion.

Even though United States strength in South Vietnam had been greatly reduced, both logistic and combat support was responsive and effective. Immediately following the initial attacks by the enemy, the United States initiated an emergency program to provide support to battered RVNAF units on all battlefields to assist them in regaining their strength and initiative. Combat support was provided by massed air and naval firepower against NVA units, their supply lines and bases.

Injected with new vigor, ARVN units resisted with determination. The enemy's desperate attempt to overwhelm our units again with his local numerical superiority was countered with B-52 and tactical air strikes. As he increased his assaults with massed infantry, the heavier his losses became. Finally, this attrition caused his offensive to run out of steam.

As long as they were given a clear mission and adequate logistic support, RVNAF units always accepted combat and fought well. During the longest and bloodiest siege of the war, the defenders of An Loc had refused to surrender. At Kontum, a fresh division was brought in for the defense of the city and it effectively drove back every enemy attack. In northern MR-1, three RVNAF divisions not only held Hue against the ferocious onslaughts of six enemy divisions but also crossed the My Chanh line to counterattack and ultimately recaptured Quang Tri City.

Equipped with effective, light-weight antitank weapons, ARVN soldiers quickly realized that they could disable the T-54 tanks whenever they came within killing range. The enemy therefore paid a high price in tanks. Our resilient soldiers also came to realize that enemy artillery could not pound them at will when the USAF responded forcefully. So they dug in and endured the siege. Most astounding was the fact that their morale did not collapse even among the less reliable RF and PF soldiers. During this time of grave emergency, Saigon also rose to the occasion by quickly replacing the ineffective, politically-appointed generals with professionals who had combat experience.

By mid-June, the RVNAF had wrested the initiative from the invaders. There was no morale collapse among the South Vietnamese population or among RVNAF troops. Well-planned U.S. airstrikes continued to take a heavy toll of NVA combat strength and the enemy had to withdraw his three badly mauled divisions from the An Loc area. The direct threat on Saigon was removed although NVA forces began to infiltrate into the Mekong Delta where they endeavored to wreck the GVN pacification achievements. In the Central Highlands, the same story was repeated. After heavy losses incurred in Kontum, the enemy retreated into the jungle to lick his wounds. In the coastal lowlands of Military Region 2, the NVA 3d Division was also dealt heavy blows during the fierce battles of May. It finally broke contact, and the ARVN forces retook the two northern districts of Binh Dinh Province.

In spite of these failures and losses the enemy continued his offensive. He injected two additional divisions into Quang Tri Province and pushed a third division into southern Military Region 1, increasing his total combat forces in this region to eight divisions, by far the greatest concentration of NVA forces in any military region during the war. He seemed poised for a big final attack against the RVN elite units north of the Hai Van Pass -- the Airborne, Marine and 1st Divisions. If he succeeded in defeating these units, Hue, the most tempting and desirable prize, would readily fall into his hands.

To obtain additional strength for this final showdown, Hanoi committed its last division which had been moved from Laos into the battle. However, NVA logistic support was no longer adequate for large scale operations due to relentless U.S. airstrikes. To oppose this formidable force on the northern frontline, South Vietnam committed its best troops whose combat effectiveness had become legend. I believe that Hanoi was convinced that if NVA forces could destroy our three elite divisions the remainder of the RVNAF could be easily defeated. Even though on the RVN side there were less troops on the line, we had the support of U.S. strategic and tactical air, naval gunfire and superior mobility. The tactical odds therefore were about even despite the fact that NVA forces always enjoyed the initiative with regard to time and place of attack.

Many observers believed that Hanoi should have acted more cautiously after NVA forces lost the initial momentum and suffered subsequent defeats. But the Hanoi leadership was stubborn and intransigent, bent as always on the most belligerant course of action. The showdown was inevitable, and Hanoi apparently believed it could win. Hanoi's easy victories during April and May seemed to confirm this belief. Gearing up for the showdown, Hanoi probably continued to think that the RVNAF would collapse and only a final blow would be necessary to hasten the process.

Another possibility that might explain Hanoi's desire for a quick victory was its concern about the political discussions which were taking place between the United States and Russia and Red China. Was it possible that Russia and China, who supplied Hanoi with nearly all its war supplies, could be persuaded by the U.S. to reduce their support in the near future?

Furthermore, a military victory during the U.S. presidential election year might inhibit the chances of the incumbent being reelected. Hanoi remembered how its 1968 offensive had affected the course of U.S. internal and international politics. Was it not possible that a Communist victory during 1972 would promote the election of a new president who would repudiate the commitment to support South Vietnam? In the final analysis, I believe this may have been Hanoi's objective for some time. In any event, the bloodiest battles of the war raged on for three months in the northernmost corner of South Vietnam.

But North Vietnam no longer had the forces needed to win. On the contrary, the odds were working against the enemy. As the fighting continued, Hanoi's chances of losing were increasing, not only militarily but also politically. Weakened and finally exhausted, the NVA forces were no match for the bolder South Vietnamese units. Contrary to the assessment of several observers, I believe that the last NVA effort in Quang Tri and Thua Thien failed to provide the enemy with any significant political advantages. Falling back in the wake of their defeat, NVA forces dispersed and switched to a less sanguine course of action: a well-orchestrated land and population grab campaign in preparation for a standstill ceasefire. And thus ended the 1972 NVA offensive.

In retrospect, Hanoi's conventional invasion of the South did not help it attain the major objectives desired. Although always the defender with an extremely disadvantageous strategic posture, South Vietnam emerged stronger than ever. Hanoi's effort had been thwarted by U.S.-RVN determination. The American response during the enemy offensive was timely, forceful and decisive. This staunch resolve of the U.S. to stand behind its ally stunned the enemy. Additionally, it brought about a strong feeling of self-assurance among the armed forces and population of South Vietnam.

Another major factor that contributed to Hanoi's military failures during 1972 was the reliability of RVNAF units. When Hanoi initiated its offensive, some had thought that it would be an ultimate test of Vietnamization and were not confident that the RVN could meet the challenge. But instead of defeat, the RVNAF had achieved quite the contrary.

Throughout the long months of the enemy offensive, the RVNAF performed like the mature, professional, dedicated fighting force it had become. Although this excellent performance was attributable to several factors, a definite tribute must be given to the U.S. advisers, especially the U.S. regional assistance commands. Even during this period of emergency, the U.S. advisory effort continued to help the RVNAF support machinery run smoothly, whether it was recruiting, equipping, training or replacing losses.

The constant input of fresh and trained manpower kept the RVNAF revitalized and helped maintain combat effectiveness in the forward areas.

The RVNAF logistic system functioned efficiently, keeping all combat units resupplied.

Intelligence collection and accurate reporting kept field commanders constantly abreast of the situation and were instrumental in formulating successful battle plans.

Improved command and control in the field also resulted in better morale for commanders and troops alike.

All of these achievements contributed to the ultimate RVNAF success in containing and defeating the most vigorous offensive North Vietnam had ever unleashed on the South and without the assistance of U.S. advisers, it would not have been possible.

The final credit for our victory should go to the individual South Vietnamese soldier, regardless of branch or service. His gallantry, courage and determination were of the highest standard. No less admirable were the sacrifices and hardships endured by the common South Vietnamese people during this long ordeal. While modern weapons might help turn the tide of a battle, they could never replace the individual soldier on the battlefield. No matter how sound a battle plan or how good a commander, our success could never had been achieved without courageous soldiers. The average South Vietnamese soldier, who grew up in war, was not only audacious and devoted to the cause for which he had been fighting but he always took pride in his career and his heart was filled with love for his family, his comrade-in-arms and his people. He was indeed a heroic warrior who represented the noblest traditions of the Vietnamese people, a most ardent patriot, and an outstanding soldier. His success during 1972 had helped forge a new national spirit of solidarity and survival that was to prevail in the post-cease-fire years.

Glossary

AO	Area of Operation
APC	Armored Personnel Carrier
ARVN	Army of the Republic of Vietnam. Common abbreviation used to refer to regular army forces to include airborne and ranger units
ARDF	Airborne Radio Direction Finding
CAV	Cavalry (U.S.)
CBU	U.S. Air Force anti-personnel bombs dropped in clusters
COSVN	Central Office for South Vietnam (Communist Party)
CP	Command Post
DMZ	Demilitarized Zone
DRAC	Delta Regional Assistance Command
FRAC	First Regional Assistance Command
FSB	Fire Support Base
FSCC	Fire Support Coordination Center
FWMA(F)	Free World Military Assistance (Forces)
GVN	Government of South Vietnam
HALO	High Altitude, Low Opening
JGS	Joint General Staff, RVNAF
LTL	Vietnamese interprovincial route (Lien Tinh Lo)
LZ	Landing Zone
LAW	Light Antitank Weapon
MACV	Military Assistance Command, Vietnam
Main Force	Viet Cong and North Vietnamese military units subordinate to COSVN, military regions, or other higher echelons of enemy command
MR	Military Region (RVN)

NVA	North Vietnamese Army
PRG	Provisional Revolutionary Government (Viet Cong)
QL	Vietnamese National Route (Quoc Lo)
RF and PF	Regional Force(s) and Popular Force(s). Military forces recruited and employed within a province
RVN	Republic of Vietnam. Sometimes used interchangeably with GVN when referring to the government or with SVN when referring to the country.
RVNAF	Republic of Vietnam Armed Forces
SAM	Surface-to-air missile
SOI	Signal Operating Instructions
SRAG	Second Regional Assistance Group
STZ	Special Tactical Zone (Biet Khu)
SVN	South Vietnam. Generally connotes the land itself
TAE	Target Acquisition Element
TAOR	Tactical Area of Responsibility
TL	Vietnamese Provincial Route (Tinh Lo)
TRAC	Third Regional Assistance Command
TOW	Tube-launched, Optically-tracked, Wire-guided (missile)
USAF	United States Air Force
VC	Viet Cong. Communist insurgents in South Vietnam
VCI	Viet Cong Infrastructure
VNAF	Vietnam Air Force

www.ingramcontent.com/pod-product-compliance
Lightning Source LLC
Chambersburg PA
CBHW080543170426
43195CB00016B/2666